SEEING IN THE DARK

Seeing in the Dark

finding God's light in the most unexpected places

NANCY ORTBERG

 Tyndale House Publishers, Inc. Carol Stream, Illinois

Visit Tyndale online at www.tyndale.com.

TYNDALE and Tyndale's quill logo are registered trademarks of Tyndale House Publishers, Inc.

Seeing in the Dark: Finding God's Light in the Most Unexpected Places

Designed by Jennifer Ghionzoli

Edited by Stephanie Rische

Library of Congress Cataloging-in-Publication Data

Ortberg, Nancy.
  Seeing in the dark : finding God's light in the most unexpected places / Nancy Ortberg.
    pages cm
  Includes bibliographical references.
  ISBN 978-1-4143-7560-1 (hc)
1. Spirituality—Christianity.   2. Light—Religious aspects—Christianity.   I. Title.
  BV4501.3.O7695 2015
  248.4—dc23   2015005719

Printed in the United States of America

21   20   19   18   17   16   15
7   6   5   4   3   2   1

To John, who brought the widening light to me . . .

Our eyes are not the only things with which we see.

Contents

Introduction

LAST MONTH JOHN AND I were in Turkey celebrating our thirtieth wedding anniversary. On one memorable day, our tour guide took us deep into a cave that was carved out more than fifteen hundred years ago by nomadic people who followed Christ, living in a land of those who did not.

It was a stumbling, slow walk in the dark. After following the path for some time, largely guided by the sound of our leader's voice and the narrow, cold walls on either side of us, we stopped.

As our eyes slowly adjusted, we saw in front of us a small room—a church—carved out of the cave centuries before. When our guide shone a slight beam from his flashlight against the walls, we were astonished by what we saw. Frescoes, painstakingly drawn by hand, still retained vivid colors of red, yellow, and blue. We saw sitting areas hewn out of rock and crosses of various designs carved into the walls. Much of the stone surface was charred black from the candles the worshippers had brought with them. This was a room where the light had burned for long periods of time. This was a room that reminded the Christ followers that there was light, even in the darkest and deepest of places.

I was struck by the intentional effort these people had applied to this one room.

Other rooms were strictly for survival. A small room carved out of the rock, five or six stories below the surface of the earth, designed for food preparation. A fire-pit area with an elaborate ventilation system. An area for milling grain. Other rooms were for sleeping, with multiple hallways connecting them for escape if necessary.

But this room was not necessary. At least not from a physical survival perspective. Yet more effort had gone into this one area than all the others combined. None of the other rooms contained art or color or symbols. In the midst of fighting for survival, these early believers had given some of their best and most time-consuming efforts to create this space to gather and worship.

This room *was* necessary. Perhaps their survival was more dependent on what they experienced in this room than on what happened in the kitchen, which kept them alive in a different way.

Our guide explained that the church had been built here because above ground, the faith community's journey was dark. They were being hunted and persecuted, so they went below ground, where it was dark as well—just a different kind of dark. Hundreds of years later, we stood on that ground below the ground, reminded that we were not the first to stumble and see in the dark. The walls continued to speak.

The references in the Bible to light in dark places are numerous. From Genesis to Revelation, light penetrates the darkness in bold and soothing ways. In the beginning, while the darkness hovered, God exploded the world into flourishing with "Let there be light." Light is offered as relief for dark paths and unknown futures. God's face is described as light[1]; his garments are a wrapping of light. God's people are called the "light of the world." God's light is so powerful in us that it can't help but leak out. Light is there—a synonym for truth and a name for Jesus. And not just a light, but the Light of the World.[2] God knows we need some.

Just as numerous are the Bible's references about the way we see in imperfect and incomplete ways, like a mirror that reflects and distorts an image at the same time. "How faint the whisper we hear of him!" Job says (Job 26:14).

And yet we are called to this journey of faith, with eyes that cannot properly focus and light that reveals only the next step. We are compelled to take that next step with merely a tug in our souls rather than the clear path we long for. We get a glimpse when what we want is a panoramic view.

What's a person to do?

Take the next step, I suppose. At least that's how it has worked—not just for me, but for most of the Christ followers I know, and as I emerged from the cave system that day, I realized that this is how it has been for Christ followers through the centuries.

Courage is putting one foot in front of the other when all you can see is a faint outline of the future. Or facing that future when it looks not at all how you'd imagined. It's having the humility to admit a wrong turn, the resilience to try again, and the grace to not let it crush you.

Faith is a funny word—it implies a gap, but we are looking to do away with that gap. We are looking for answers carved in stone, and we get a word. We are searching for certainty, and we get mystery and reflection. We think we would be safe in certainty, and yet it eludes us. We want enormous floods of light, and we get a flicker.

A majestic scene in nature stirs something deep within us that cannot be explained by factor analysis. And the things that can be explained do not grip us at the same level. We have such hopes for our lives and our loved ones; then a tragedy hits, and nothing is ever the same. Yet over time, joy and hope and beauty raise a tiny tendril of faith back into our lives, and we cannot explain it. We are seeing in the dark.

Perhaps that is most of what our faith journey is. Scripture seems to be full of stories of that ilk—of people who took the next step when they were trembling in the shadows. Yet somewhere between when we read those stories and when we are left to imagine them, they take on a quality of assuredness that is simply not there. From Genesis to Revelation, God's people have been asked to take the next step when they cannot see the next step. That's the invitation you and I have been given as well.

Right around one year old, each of our three children began their first attempts at walking. For the few months before, they had been in various stages of crawling and pulling themselves up. Mobility seemed to compel them onward, even when their initial tries landed them in frustration or falls.

Their chubby little hands would grasp something just a bit higher than they were, and with comical wobbliness, they would pull themselves upright in jerky movements. With the great confidence that being upright seemed to instill, they would take that first step. A small, slow smile would spread across their faces, but they were not really walking yet.

A few days later, buoyed by a measure of success, they would let loose the support they had gripped so tightly, and high kneed and unsteady, precarious and tottering, they would take their first few unaided steps before tumbling down.

From an outsider's view, as far as walking goes? Pretty unimpressive.

From a coaching view? So much wrong—probably not even worth a coaching session. This toddler is not a player. Walking? Not in his future. Probably ought not to give up his day job.

Their movements were precarious and unbalanced, and it took only two or three steps before complete failure. So staccato were the motions, their "walking" looked nothing like the real thing. Recommendation: continue crawling.

But as parents? We cheered as if they had scored the winning touchdown, like they'd received the first-place math award, like they'd just landed on the moon. We had hope. We knew the next time would be a little better, and with enough next times, those kids would be walking. And when they could walk, they could go places—for the rest of their lives. There was enough potential in that first "all wrong" step that our joy seemed warranted.

Such a discrepancy. Such an enormous gap between what we saw that day and what we imagined could be possible. Such hope in a tiny, wobbly, unimpressive first step. But such a deep belief that, with encouragement, cheers, practice, and rest, our toddler would walk. There was little to no evidence. Just a tiny flicker of light. A possibility worth banking on.

Our oldest daughter, Laura, was thirteen months old when she took her first unaided steps. We were sitting on the floor in my in-laws' small kitchen. My mother-in-law, Kathy, was holding Laura up, facing me. I called to Laura and held out my hands. Kathy unfurled her fingers from Laura, and Laura took four Frankenstein-like steps before I scooped her up in my arms. You would have thought Laura had won the Nobel Peace Prize from the celebration that followed.

That night, after her bath, we snuggled Laura into her flannel jammies with the feet and sang to her. We rocked her in the rocking chair in the nursery and read her a book as she sipped the last bit of milk from her Tommee Tippee cup. Kissing the soft part of her neck, I laid Laura in her crib with her favorite blankie and whispered, "Good night, little walker."

Later, before we went to bed, I gently opened the door to the nursery and stood over Laura's crib. She was fast asleep, her head turned to the side, a pink flush in her cheeks. The hair on the back of her neck was curled into ringlets, which often happened when she was warm. Her lips moved in a sucking motion, and her breathing was deep and even. As I looked at her, with the moonlight casting patterns on the sheets from the stencil-like effect of the lace curtains, I thought my heart would explode in my chest. There was so much love. A universe of love. Love—way more than could possibly be contained in my body—and yet there it was, deep inside, expanding and threatening to blow me apart. In that sacred quiet, the only sound was a baby and a mother breathing.

I placed my hand on Laura's tummy—firm enough to feel her, light enough not to wake her—and I prayed. A simple prayer, a short one. "May her faltering steps be strong; may she walk into her future with you, God."

My hope in that prayer was that what we'd seen that day would grow. That the glimpse we'd had would abound into more. That she would walk—physically, metaphorically— into her future with God.

What gives us such hope in such a small thing? Or per- haps that's backward. Perhaps it is the nature of hope that it must start with small things. Or no things. Or in the dark. Otherwise, it wouldn't be hope.

So hope began. Even in the smallest of things, even in the cells that were growing inside me when I had my positive home pregnancy test with Laura. Even with that first step.

And as her life unfolded, the hope would burgeon and open, and horizons would expand into her future.

But what about as life comes toward its end? As the expanse narrows and what is left ahead shrinks, what then? This is the natural progression of divergence and convergence. . . .

Last week I sat at Joyce Brandle's bedside. She and her husband, Ed, have been longtime attenders of our church—more than forty years. Ed is an usher at our church, and nearly every Sunday he greets me with a gentle hug. He's been a deacon and a Marine. There is, I think, a connection. He and Joyce have been married for more than fifty years, and they live just a few blocks from us. Joyce is dying of bile duct cancer. She was diagnosed four months ago, and the doctors told them both that there was nothing they could do for her, that she had probably about a year to live.

So I stopped by. I brought a small glass jar with a few roses cut from our yard. I rang the doorbell, and Ed, moving slowly, answered. He was in the living room watching football while Joyce was in their bedroom resting.

I waited while Ed went to check on Joyce, and he returned to tell me she was awake and would welcome a visit. Their house reminded me of my grandmother's home back when I was a child. The decor and design were reminiscent of the fifties—not much had changed. It was comforting in that way memory can be.

I made my way down the hall and to the bedroom where

Joyce lay on top of the bedspread with a blanket over her thin body, her Persian cat curled up in the nook of her knees. Joyce was emerging from her nap, but her sky-blue eyes were sharp and clear. Her mouth was dry, and she fought with her lips as they caught on her teeth before she was able to greet me. She took a sip of water as I sat down, and her face lit up when she saw the small cluster of roses I placed at her bedside.

For the next half hour Joyce and I had a delightful conversation. She asked questions about my family, and I asked about hers. We talked about her health and her cat. "She knows something is wrong. She typically wouldn't stay this close to me all day, but she won't leave my side whether I'm sleeping or awake."

She told me that hospice was coming once or twice a week, just to help with transferring from her bed to a chair and with taking a bath. Whenever it was, years ago, that little blue-eyed Joyce had taken her first faltering steps, she was coming quickly to the end of that ability. Her walking days were largely behind her now. Her world was narrow: the four walls of this bedroom, the view of the backyard through the sliding glass doors across from her bed. Even the outdoors, for the most part, was now beyond her.

"I'm not afraid," she said.

Ed interrupted us a couple of times, offering something to eat or drink—the loving offerings of a devoted and bereft husband. The kindness was palpable.

"I'm not afraid."

And for the next few minutes, her countenance and the

cadence of her words supported that bold statement. She talked about how grateful she was to know Jesus. Her world was narrowing, her steps gone. This world was becoming more and more dark and distant. And the light—it was before her. It was Jesus.

Those were rich minutes, with me mostly listening, trying to absorb. Then she asked about a family from our church whose sixteen-year-old son had just taken his own life. It had wrenched our community, and she had heard about it. I related the few details I knew about this unthinkable incident.

Then here's what Joyce said: "It won't be long until I am with God, maybe a few months. I think the first thing I'd like to do is to find Evan. And when I see him, I'm going to scold him. I cannot imagine how his parents will ever be the same again. But then, much longer than I scold him, I'm going to hold him. And I'm going to hold him and hold him and hold him. And I'm going to keep him close by until his parents see him again."

From the outside looking at Joyce, it seems like her light is narrowing and the dark is before her. But hearing what is coming from inside her? Maybe not. Maybe she is moving toward what looks to us like a thin stream of light about to be snuffed out, but in reality is an ever-widening band of light. And as she walks toward it, it is actually about to open up to her an eternity of nothing but light.

CHAPTER 1

Dark Skies

I have loved the stars too fondly to be fearful of the night.

SARAH WILLIAMS

THE INTERNATIONAL DARK-SKY ASSOCIATION is a group dedicated to the preservation of our globe's night sky. It works to reduce light pollution, solely for the purpose of allowing us to gaze into the "extraordinary wonders of the nighttime sky." One of the many places set aside as a dark-sky region is Death Valley. Though Los Angeles and Death Valley are only a four-hour drive apart, the contrast is so remarkable you'd think there were two different skies.

In the city, with all the competing lights, you may be able to pick out only a handful of stars overhead. In Death Valley, it's another world. The sky is smudged with bands of silver-white; dazzling twinkles radiate from millions of miles away. It is another sky, yet the same one. The dark is what allows you to see.

My first memory of the wonders that the dark sky holds is from when I was seven years old. It was the first summer of many that my mom and dad and I vacationed in the White Mountains of Arizona. Tucked against the New Mexico border, at an elevation of more than eight thousand feet, this area was dazzling. Green meadows between tall peaks, plunging river canyons, purple wildflowers, and German brown trout in the streams.

We stayed at the Sprucedale Guest Ranch, a family-owned "guest dude ranch." Actually, it was a working cattle ranch, and in the summer they supplemented their income by opening their doors to guests. We stayed in handmade log cabins that ran electricity for two hours in the morning and a few more at night. Meals were in the ranch house—unbelievable homemade, fresh creations—and the daily activities were fishing, hiking, and horseback riding. The horseback riding included finding and driving in the cattle that were feeding at the higher elevations. A couple of times during the week, in the afternoons, we were in the corral, roping and branding the calves.

The first night we stayed there, we were sitting on the front porch of our cabin. As my eyes adjusted to the dark sky, I couldn't quite comprehend what I was seeing. My dad, noticing the quizzical look on my face, said, "That's the Milky Way."

For the next few minutes we alternated between awe-filled

silence and conversation as he explained to me the vast number of heavenly bodies in the sky that in LA had gone unseen.

He pointed out tiny dots of light that when connected (at least by the imagination) made up the outlines of mythological creatures the ancients had seen and named. He told me about the navigational abilities these stars and planets had given to the Polynesians, the Vikings, and sailors from many lands since. He also talked about our place in all of this vastness. Small but connected.

Stories, direction, place—all above my head, but largely unseen until it was dark. Very dark.

It took time for my eyes to adjust, to be able to see in the dark. When there is a low-light condition, the pupils automatically dilate in order to let in more light. It's like taking your first step into a dark movie theater and trying to find a seat. It's so dark you're not sure there even are seats. But just a minute or so later, with time and adjustment, you see what you could not see before.

When I was a little girl my parents split up. Not an uncommon story, you'd think, but this was in the early 1960s. I was, quite literally, the *only* kid in my elementary school whose parents were going through a divorce. I know, because occasionally I heard teachers whispering to one another as I walked down the hallways, "That's her; she's the one." There was no unkind tone—it was just such an anomaly.

I was in third grade, eight years old. Some of my strongest

and most painful memories from that time were the fights before they split. The yelling was awful, and I would alternate between trying to push my way between them to get them to stop and running to the den and turning the television volume up loud enough to drown out the noise. The noise terrified me because when it went on long enough, one of them would leave.

One parent would drive away in the car, and the other, probably exhausted from the ordeal, would collapse into bed. But that's not where I went. I crawled onto the kitchen counter and peered through the curtains, watching and waiting for the parent who had left to come back.

It's remarkable how vivid that experience is to this day. My recall, not always my strongest suit, is impeccable when it comes to those evenings. I can still feel the cold turquoise counter tiles on my shins. I can picture the fabric of the kitchen curtains with their teakettle design. The thick brass hooks on the curtains made a peculiar sound against the rod when I pushed them aside, searching for the familiar headlights that would mean my mom or dad was home.

When I saw the car pulling into our one-lane driveway, I would return the curtains to their closed position and run to my bed, pretending to be asleep and listening for the turn of the kitchen door. Once the parent who had driven away was back, I felt such a strong relief that sleep would overtake me.

Interestingly, my parents ended up reconciling a year later, and until the day my father died in 1990, they were together. But it took me years of counseling, talking through things with friends, and wrestling with God to understand the full impact all of this had on me. There were long seasons, especially through high school and college, when I found it laughable that it had affected me at all. Perhaps those years of denial explain why it took so long before this issue bubbled to the surface and I was finally forced to look at it.

There's one other thing I remember from this time. An occasional, faint whisper. Not even a whisper, really—more a soul presence. Every once in a while, on that cold tile counter, along with the terror I felt, there was an accompanying presence—a sense that I was *not* as alone as it seemed. The small awareness that I was not on my own.

In Hebrew, the word *psalm* means "book of praise." The problem is, once you open the book of Psalms, you realize that well over half of the chapters are psalms of *lament*. Hardly truth in advertising . . .

So the one book of the Bible that invites us into its pages by promising birds chirping and flowers blooming is filled with words like *despair*, *alone*, *wicked*, and *loathing*. Far more plentiful than the verses that remind us to rejoice and praise are those that admit to distance from and doubts about God.

Imagine if your responsive reading in church next Sunday were taken from Psalm 58:

Break the teeth in their mouths, O God. . . .
Let them vanish like water that flows away. . . .

> May they be like a slug that melts away as it
>> moves along,
>> like a stillborn child that never sees the sun.

Or Psalm 88:

> I am set apart with the dead, . . .
> whom you remember no more. . . .
> You have put me in the lowest pit,
>> in the darkest depths. . . .
> I am confined and cannot escape;
>> my eyes are dim with grief. . . .
> I cry to you for help, . . .
> Why, LORD, do you reject me
>> and hide your face from me? . . .
>> Darkness is my closest friend.

All the voices speaking aloud, in unison. Hard to picture, isn't it? But these verses are the holy words of Scripture coming to us. The implication is clear: right alongside the psalms of praise—good news, triumph, and joy—are the harsh words of woundedness, fear, and despair. Perhaps they even imply that the way to praise is through lament, not by avoiding pain or pretending it doesn't hurt so bad.

In fact, before you read any further, go back to the two passages above and read them aloud. Read them slowly, deliberately, and with meaning.

Well? There are some seriously harsh sentiments in there.

It's raw, it's rude, it's childish—it's the Bible. As you read these passages aloud, can you see that there has been some time when these words were an honest commentary on your own life? Maybe that time is now.

Either way, the writers of the psalms are trying to tell us that it's all part of the journey. But what happens is that we don't like that message, so we plaster on a strained smile and talk about victory and peace, when neither is around for miles. The very fact that we *never* do responsive readings in our churches with these kinds of passages points to our denial of the hard stuff and our superficial comfort with frosting and quick, easy answers as a substitute for the rough edges of faith.

Someone once said that faith is not a personal possession until you have suffered. That person understood that the very nature of faith requires the grit and courage to be in the dark so you can eventually see in the dark. Then faith becomes faith.

To get to the perspective reflected in Psalm 58 and Psalm 88, there has to be some gut-wrenching pain. Betrayal. Woundedness. Fear. Terror. Anger. Fury. Jaw-dropping disappointment. Loss. Death. Separation.

A good friend of mine lost her child recently. Unspeakable, seismic sadness. When she called, I listened in stunned silence as she told me what had happened. My mind was racing, trying to comprehend the reality of it and thinking about getting a plane ticket as soon as I hung up the phone.

I had received the phone call just as I'd pulled up to our house, and I sat in my car long after we hung up, crying in disbelief and pain for my friend. For the next few days, before I left for the funeral, I wondered, *Who else?*

As I walked through crowds at the store and went to meetings at work, I thought, *Who else near me has been through this kind of horror and buries it below the surface because no one wants to see this kind of pain up close?* Were there scores of people I was rubbing elbows with who were a part of this club that no one wanted to join, but I just couldn't see it?

I remember when one of my friends had a miscarriage, she was amazed by the women who came out of the woodwork with "me too." She'd had no idea. One of the rules of membership was silence until another member was recognized.

At the funeral, I watched my friend's face. It was taut and worn, somewhere between aging and lost. I had known her face since we were in junior high school. We had been children together ourselves. Now she had lost hers. Lost. And she looked like a toddler who realized for the first time that it was possible to lose your favorite toy or even break it, and no one—no one—could find it or fix it. Terror and unspeakable sadness.

I wish there were another answer. Sometimes you just have to sit and stay in the darkness. Sit and stay when every cell in your body is telling you to move and medicate. Sit and stay, wait. Let the dark sky envelope you, because if you move too quickly, your eyes will never adjust, and if they never adjust, they will never see. At least they'll never see what they are supposed to see.

Sit and stay and wait. Let the talking of friends subside, let the silence deafen, let the pain overwhelm, and wait. If you don't, you will miss it. You will not hear the whisper or see the flicker. You will be moving and unable to receive what you need most.

There is a new reality that takes time to see. Not exactly a new reality, but a more real one that only comes into focus in silence. A reality that is best seen through eyes filled with tears. A seemingly dark sky, which after a bit of time reveals the magnificent Milky Way.

In the garden of Gethsemane when Jesus was arrested, a period of darkness was beginning. "This is your hour— when darkness reigns" (Luke 22:53). And between that moment and the morning of the Resurrection, there was deep darkness. A darkness during which Jesus kept mostly still. There was no fight. He gave Herod "no answer" (Luke 23:9). While Peter sprang into action, chopping off an ear and vehemently denying he knew Jesus, Jesus was still. He went where he was led. He knew the darkness had started, and he let it envelop him. Perhaps because he knew that *through* this darkness was the only way *to* the light.

CHAPTER 2

The Shadow of Death

Jesus wept.

JOHN 11:35

MY GIRLS AND I LEFT AT SEVEN O'CLOCK on a Sunday morning for our road trip. There are few things I love more. We made it all the way to Bakersfield before Laura said, "I don't think I can stand one more trip over the Grapevine. Let's take the back roads." And with a navigation click on my phone, we were traveling through hill country, stopping for lunch in Tehachapi, then driving through Mojave as the land gave way to the high desert before turning to the mountain forest.

Our destination? Lake Gregory, nestled in the mountains just outside of Los Angeles. The occasion? Emily's wedding.

Emily and my daughter Mallory had been close friends since they were eight years old and going into second grade, when we had just moved to the Chicago area. Mallory and Emily had giggled their way through the years together, even going to the same college. And now Emily had met Greg, and the party was on.

We'd had July 14 on our calendar for months, ever since the engagement. But now, on our way down, meandering through the small towns and deeply textured land, we knew we weren't headed for a wedding. The party was still on, but it would be only a reception. Three months earlier, Emily and her wedding party had headed from California back home to Chicago so her father could walk her down the aisle. Ron's doctor had determined that Ron wouldn't make it till July.

So July became April; the honeymoon was postponed since both Emily and Greg were teachers and in the middle of a school year; and the original wedding date became a reception, minus one.

They handled it with such a winsome combination of grace and grief. In those three months, life did not unfold as planned, and what was supposed to be the happiest three months of Emily's life . . . wasn't. Bridesmaids and grooms-men hurriedly packed suitcases and grabbed flights. Family members moved their lives around. And on a quiet evening in April, Ron, with an oxygen tube in his nose and a suit that may have fit months before but now just hung on him, walked his daughter down the aisle. His countenance was alternately somber and beaming. During the father-daughter dance that followed the ceremony, Ron and Emily touched foreheads.

At the July 14 reception, Emily and Greg showed video

clips of the wedding. There wasn't a dry eye in the room. Chris, Emily's delightful brother, was audibly sobbing while reaching over to hold his mom's hand.

Just a few minutes later, when the dinner was finished and the dancing had begun, Chris hit the dance floor in a way that would have made Channing Tatum proud.

How is that possible? In one person's heart, deepest grief. His heart was torn, ripped, numb, and devastated. And it was expansive, full, whole, and alive. There was unmistakable and unmitigated *joy*.

Apart from God, I think you can experience that, but I'm not sure you can adequately explain it. It just doesn't make sense. One should definitely preclude the other. How is it possible for one heart to hold such disparate worlds?

This life is simply a setup for pain. Created for perfection yet living in a broken world, designed for an eternity that is mostly veiled, you and I are caught between what could be and what is. Every longing and ache we feel is a sign of that gap. In that gap is room for such a multitude of competing experiences that war within us. And in that gap is where God lives.

When we think about the abundant life that Jesus came to invite us into, pain seems like something to avoid or minimize. Many Christians have honed denial to an art form, and as a result, chirpy and clueless sentences come out of their mouths—words that seem to defy reality.

But we are not called to create a "fantasy faith." One of my favorite comments from Dallas Willard reminds us that God works exclusively in reality: "God has yet to bless anyone except where they actually are, and if we faithlessly discard situation after situation, moment after moment, as not being 'right,' we will simply have no place to receive his kingdom into our life."[1]

I had those words printed on a small card that I have slipped into the pages of my Bible. I read them often because I am so tempted to fight reality, to look for a better day, to want to choose either grief or joy because that clarity makes things easier.

Ironically, however, living in reality, embracing pain, may be one of the deepest and most profound ways to the abundant life. And the juxtaposition of pain with any opposite experience—joy, gratitude, love, peace, contentedness—may initially put our brains on tilt, but eventually it has the power to take us exactly where we need to be.

Pain pressurizes us. Whether it's small, medium, or large, pain comes to us in the form of doubt, sorrow, disappointment, tragedy, and annoyance. It brings to the surface what we have a tendency to overlook, disregard, or ignore.

Joy is the contrast. It's a completely different experience, existing in the same space, or at least side by side. Chris's tears, followed by his impressive dance skills.

This in-between space is where God meets us and grows us in our understanding of who he is. Only tested faith is a personal possession. As uncomfortable as it is, when we surrender to live in these gaps and in these contrasts, we allow God to do his most profound work in us.

This rhythm of Jesus—leaning in, going deep in times of great pain—also mirrors the rhythms of God throughout time. From the beginning of creation, in times of human disobedience, sin, willful withdrawal, and apathy, God is at work, re-forming our misguided pictures of who he is. He is patient in our pain.

Perhaps one of the best illustrations of this is in John 11. This is the passage where Jesus raises his friend Lazarus from the dead. An impressive story, to say the least, but just under the surface of the story we are so familiar with, there is much more going on.

The chapter begins by telling us that a man named Lazarus, whose sisters happened to be Mary and Martha of Luke 10 fame, was sick. Most likely, all three of them were part of the group of about seventy or so people, in addition to the twelve apostles, who often traveled with Jesus—learning from him, taking care of necessary daily tasks for the band of followers, and financially funding the travel.

The sisters sent a message to Jesus. It was simple and urgent: "Lord, the one you love is sick" (John 11:3).

And while there is no other wording to the message, just the fact that they sent someone more than twenty miles to deliver it spoke volumes. In the ancient world, a twenty-mile journey was an epic trek, undertaken only in times of great necessity. They wanted Jesus to come. They wanted Jesus to make things better.

When he heard what was happening, Jesus said aloud, most likely for the sake of his disciples, "This sickness will not end in death, but God will be glorified through it" (John 11:4, my paraphrase).

Then John records something strange. He writes, "When he heard that Lazarus was sick, he stayed where he was two more days" (John 11:6). I'm quite certain that wasn't the response Mary and Martha were hoping for. It seems to have made such an impression on the disciples that John recorded it. I'm guessing they were, at the very least, scratching their heads.

And I'm guessing that Mary and Martha were scanning the horizon every day for the telltale cloud of dust that would indicate Jesus was coming. I imagine that they comforted each other at each sunset, saying, "He'll be here tomorrow."

Picking up in verse 17, John tells us that when Jesus finally arrived, Lazarus had already been in the tomb for four days. If we do the math, we can gather that Lazarus was most likely dead by the time Jesus received the message. Then Jesus waited two full days before setting out on the twenty-mile walk. Yep, Lazarus was dead.

Before Jesus could make his way into the town of Bethany, Martha broke away from the large group of people that had traveled from Jerusalem (about two miles away) to be with Mary and Martha in their grief and mourning.

One of the subtle, secondary points in this passage is how each of the sisters reacted, completely in keeping within their personalities, as established in Luke 10. Martha, the outspoken activist, quickly left the mourners in her home and ran to meet Jesus. The first thing she said to him was, "Lord . . . if you had been here, my brother would not have died" (John 11:21).

Then Martha, in what seems like a quick recovery, so as not to sound too accusatory, added, "But I know that even now God will give you whatever you ask" (John 11:22).

Martha still wasn't clear on who Jesus was. There was a vast separation between Jesus and God in her mind. She knew that Jesus could get God to respond to his requests; she had seen that before. But her words betrayed her lack of understanding. She didn't realize that Jesus wasn't simply another great teacher and spiritual man, closely connected to the heavenly Father.

And while, given the situation, Jesus ought to have been moving rapidly to where Lazarus was, he stopped and took the time to go a little deeper, to stretch Martha's mind and heart, to move her a little closer to a true understanding of his nature.

Jesus told Martha that her brother would rise again. Martha gave the pat Sunday-school answer: "Yes, I know that in the resurrection, my brother Lazarus will rise again" (John 11:24, my paraphrase).

Then Jesus said words that provided a clear affirmation of who he is: "I am the resurrection and the life. The one who believes in me will live, even though they die; and whoever lives by believing in me will never die. Do you believe this?" (John 11:25-26).

Honestly, couldn't we have this conversation later? Perhaps over some tea and a meal, after you have fixed our tragedy with Lazarus? It was almost as if Jesus thought that helping her understand more clearly who he was and what was going on was as important as her brother's death.

Jesus wasn't testing her belief to see if she would qualify to have her brother resurrected. Knowing that in her grief, her soul was open in a way not typical, he was taking the time to help her know more deeply what reality was—what it is.

That's a *really* important distinction. This was not a test; this was an opportunity. This moment with Martha was as priceless to Jesus, and as worth stopping for, as his next act of raising Lazarus would be.

Jesus got really clear with Martha: "I am the resurrection and the life. The one who believes in me will live, even though they die; and whoever lives by believing in me will never die" (John 11:25-26). Jesus clarified that he was not just a really amazing prophet, an astounding teacher, a holy man of the highest order. He was I Am.

Then he said simply, "Do you believe this?" (John 11:26).

Martha affirmed her belief that Jesus was the Messiah, the long-promised Son of God. The I Am of Exodus 3.

Then, Mary. She ran out to meet Jesus after Martha had returned to the house and told Mary he was asking for her. She was followed by the multitude of mourners, who upon seeing her rush out of the room assumed she was returning to the tomb to mourn her brother.

Mary fell at Jesus' feet and said the same thing her sister had said: "Lord, if you had been here, my brother would not have died" (John 11:32).

Now the next six verses (33-38) pack in a *lot* of story. In just a few words, Jesus went from a calm posture of teaching to being "deeply moved in spirit and troubled" (John 11:33). All this because of what he saw . . .

Mary weeping. Along with all those who were mourning with her. The grief was overwhelming and troubling. And it stirred something deep in the soul of Jesus.

It couldn't have been that he was simply sorrowful over the death of his friend Lazarus. He knew that in just a minute or two, Lazarus would be alive. Something much deeper was going on.

The word John uses here is deeply descriptive. Nothing in the narrative can fully explain this shift in Jesus' spirit. After all, Mary said the same sentence her sister had said just minutes before.

But John, who by this time deeply knew the face of Jesus, saw something come over him that was noteworthy. My guess is that only John noticed the change of countenance. The word he uses to describe Jesus' reaction is *embrimaomai*.

John had seen this look on Jesus' face before, but only on occasion.[2] Yet in this passage, in verses 33 and 38, John uses it *twice*.

This word paints a picture of an agitated animal—snorting, nostrils flaring. It implies indignation, turmoil, agitation, and anger—a caged hostility. And this reaction seems to come in response to the deep sorrow Mary and the others were experiencing over the death of their dear brother and friend Lazarus.

Jesus' soul was wrenched when he saw what sin and brokenness and death had done to the people he had created and loved. Imagine Jesus at Creation, with such hopes and dreams for this perfect world he'd made. The disappointment—the gap between what he'd imagined and what sin had done to that dream—must have been more than he could stand. And it wasn't just sorrow he felt. His reaction went much deeper than that. It tapped into anger. Near rage. This was *his* world. And here was all this brokenness and woundedness around him. The people he'd designed for flourishing and love were devastated and hopeless. The world he had created for beauty and perfection was cracked and marred.

Tears slipped down his face. Verse 35 says that Jesus wept. Not wailed (*klaio*), like the piercing sounds of the mourners. But *dakryo*, the quiet sadness that wells up, the sorrow that forms tears.

And somewhere between the rage and the sorrow, Jesus came to the tomb. John tells us that the tomb had a stone across the entrance, which Jesus asked to have removed. This was a scene that would be replayed with Jesus on the other side of the stone in just a short time.

Martha (let's not miss that this wonderful woman spoke out of who she was) reminded Jesus that if they did that, the smell would clear out the area, seeing as Lazarus had been dead for four days. No matter which embalming practices of the day had been used, it was not going to be pretty.

Undeterred, Jesus had them remove the stone. Then, before any of the Lazarus drama, Jesus prayed a pretty funny prayer. Basically: "Okay, Father, now before you bring Lazarus out, I'm going to pray out loud so everyone standing here can hear me. You and I both know I'm not doing this for my sake, but I'd like for these folks to get it" (see John 11:41-42).

After this prayer, Jesus called to Lazarus to come out. And after all this buildup—some forty-three verses—John simply records that Lazarus came out and Jesus told the folks to remove his grave clothes.

No time is spent describing the amazement, disbelief, awe, and celebration that inevitably followed. To drive home the main point, John omits that part to focus on the frustration Jesus felt as he walked to the tomb. The gap. The space between what could be and what was. The painful distance between perfection and reality.

That space, that place, where most of life is lived. And here, Jesus lingered.

And here it is that he lingers with us. We are in a rush to get over and through it. Understandably. And yet here is our life. Right in that uncomfortable space. We want out, and he wants in.

CHAPTER 3

Through the Cracks

We take the stability of the earth for granted, but in reality, the ground we walk across and build structures on is constantly shifting. The motions of the planet's crust usually happen too slowly for us to notice. But sometimes the ground seems to take a jump, setting in motion events that topple buildings, send oceans lurching, and change the landscape.

EXPLORATORIUM.EDU

WALKING AROUND THE FIELD IN OLEMA, you wouldn't initially notice anything out of the ordinary. It's a beautiful meadow, the kind you get used to when you grow up in California. It's springtime, and wildflowers dot the grass, punctuating it with the vivid orange of poppies and the deep purple of lupine. Mother and baby sheep are grazing there, and a gentle wind is blowing. It's so close to the ocean that you can detect the faint smell of salt in the air, but with the coastal hills, you can't quite catch a view.

Over to one side is a narrow, dry riverbed.

But eventually you realize it's not a riverbed at all. If you look closely at the sign that marks the trailhead, it will educate you that you are actually walking on the San Andreas Fault line. It is exceedingly deceptive: what looks like a dry riverbed is actually the small outward expression of a deep inner-earth reality. There is a crack in the planet, and you are currently straddling it.

Cracks are bad enough in your favorite crystal glass, your iPhone screen, or your car windshield. Most of us are hoping to avoid them in our planet. There's no quick fix for these cracks, no repair or replacement service; we just have to live with them—and their repercussions. Growing up in Southern California, you know that.

It was hard to imagine that what I was seeing out in a field in Olema was directly linked to my earthquake experiences in the Los Angeles area. As a kid, I definitely got used to the smaller ones—a little shaking, a little shifting, and it was over. Almost fun. Folks might stop to look up for a moment, nodding at one another to communicate that we knew what we were experiencing, and then mindlessly returning to what we'd been doing when it started.

But when the Richter number started to move up a bit—say, five or higher—and the shaking and lurching didn't stop quickly enough, things changed. People started looking for doorways to stand under and thinking that before the next one, they really needed to put together that earthquake preparedness kit they'd read about in the newspaper.

The higher on the Richter scale, the longer the shaking lasts, and the closer you are to the epicenter, the more likely you are to sit up and take note, to feel the fear rising. In 1971 the

Sylmar earthquake struck, registering at 6.6. On a scale of one to ten, 6.6 doesn't sound much worse than a 5.0, but with this scale, every one-tenth reflects a tenfold increase of the power.

The earthquake caused millions of dollars in damage, and sixty-four people died. I was a teenager, so I slept through it, awakening to my mother shaking me. I think her shake was a 7.2 . . .

In 1994, the Northridge earthquake hit. It was early in the morning and most of LA was in bed when it registered a whopping 6.7. Strongest alarm clock ever—a collective awakening for an entire metropolitan area. The quake resulted in billions of dollars in damage, and fifty-seven people died. I was no longer a teenager; I was a mother of three small children, and my husband and I ran quickly to their bedrooms. I think I actually pulled a small plug of hair out of Mallory's head as I tried to wake her up to get her under a doorframe. I guess it's genetic.

The shaking went on for at least thirty seconds—an eternity when you don't know if it is diminishing or escalating. When it was over, we pulled the kids into bed with us, waiting to see if there would be immediate aftershocks, then turned on the news. Ironically, that was the day we'd planned on taking our kids to Knott's Berry Farm. As the initial emotion settled down, that was the first question they asked: Would we still be going? Having grown up in SoCal, I immediately realized this could quite possibly be the best day ever to go. A few hours later, we were zipping onto rides with absolutely no one in line. A memorable day indeed.

I was out of state when the Loma Prieta earthquake rocked the San Francisco Bay Area in 1989. Oddly enough, as a second-generation Californian, it was hard to be away from my state when this happened. I read about the collapse of the Nimitz Freeway and the heroic rescue of people trapped in apartment rubble. At the time, thousands of people were in Candlestick Park for the third game of the World Series, and injuries might have been much higher if the quake had hit earlier and those folks had been on the freeways traveling to the game.

When we moved to Chicago, so many Midwesterners said to me, "Well, I'll bet you're glad to be in a land with no earthquakes!"

I didn't have the heart to tell them that while fifty-seven people died in the strongest earthquake I experienced, the first summer I lived in Chicago more than eight hundred people died from the heat. Or that I feared seven-month winters much more than seventy-nine-second earthquakes . . .

But I knew what they meant. There's something pretty disturbing when terra firma becomes terra shake-a. When the ground beneath your feet—the one thing you can count on as being solid—isn't. At least with a tornado there are a few seconds to push the siren and get to the basement, but earthquakes hit without warning.

I think our souls have fault lines too. For the most part you can't see them from the outside—they are deep and hidden. But forces we may not even be aware of are exerting stress and pressure until these lines slip against each other and cause everything to move. And we never even see it coming.

When I was in graduate school I was in love with a guy. He loved me too. That's fodder for a pretty good story right there. But as usual, there was more to it than that. We had dated for a few months in our hometown, but by fall, because of school, we shifted to long distance. And there were some good things about that setup as well. For a time, you can really learn a lot about a person from being separated. We wrote long letters, talked on the phone, and scheduled visits when we could afford it.

After a couple of years, it became one of those situations where we had dated long enough that we needed to decide: Do we get engaged or do we break up? It didn't look like the long-distance thing was going to resolve itself, so I resolved myself to weigh in: we needed to break up.

It made sense on paper, but I think I underestimated the emotional toll the breakup would incur. Three months later we spoke face-to-face. He had been sad when we broke up. Now I broached the subject of getting back together, and he didn't want to. Now I was sad.

Except I didn't yet know that *sad* didn't even begin to describe it. It was like God used this event in my life to open up the cracks in my soul that were deep below the surface, deep below even this relationship.

I experienced six months of upheaval, chaos, and aftershocks way out of proportion to this one event, as devastating as it was. One hundred eighty-one days of inner turmoil and pain, weight loss, and tears. Constant conversations with friends, as if by my words I could stay tethered to the very earth I felt myself floating away from.

My inner being was a swirl of questions, fears, and pain. Who was I? Where was God? I thought I'd heard him so clearly in regard to this person.

I had no appetite; I was preoccupied with my heart but had to work and study; I was insecure about myself; I felt despair about the future; I mistrusted my own choices; I felt indescribable pain about my parents' splitting up when I was eight (where did *that* come from?); I was afraid of being alone; I worried that I wasn't good enough to be anyone's lifelong partner; I feared I was irreparably damaged but no one had the courage to tell me; I wondered where I could get the help I needed when I wasn't sure what that even was . . .

The pain of the one thing shattered open the pain of a hundred hidden things. Only God saw the connection at the time.

And there were, in my life, even more seismic shifts than this breakup. Before this, being a little girl—an only child— and being terrified by my parents' fights. After this, being tested for multiple sclerosis and adding to all of the above fears those of incapacity and physical dependence. After I got married, wondering if I would be able to have children. My list could go on, and I'm guessing you have started yours. What we have in common is how, when life shatters, we have a chance to grow deep.

God, more deeply aware than we are of the cracks in our

souls, uses these seismic shifts to form us into the people we long to be. Like the relief efforts that follow an earthquake, he helps us sort out the issues, name them, follow their threads, and use the pain to build an identity in him—something that never shakes.

Even at my age, I don't hope for an earthquake. But I understand the ways earthquakes relieve the stress deep in the earth. After going through so many, I know that they are the starting place for healing—often for things I wasn't even aware were in need of healing. Perhaps part of the gift of the quake is that very realization.

I find myself surprised by the insecurity that still lingers—that doesn't often show up on the outside but apparently is deeply rooted inside. I'm amazed to find that impatience or a critical spirit is buried deep within me, and without the cracks formed by the shifting of my soul, I might have gone on for years thinking I had that issue conquered.

I don't often feel lonely, but in all the turmoil of that season, I experienced a kind of separation from others that was painful and scary. I still find that I get the big things mixed up with the good things, that I spend much of my life living for the approval of others, and that I have anger, jealousy, and fear that I mask as leadership, competence, and confidence.

That's not to say that God and I haven't spent years working on all this stuff. We have. But each time my soul cracks open, there is an invitation from him to a deeper journey into those familiar broken places.

But that's not all. These earthquakes in my life—they are

not just about the bad stuff. To be sure, at first it seems like that's all there is. Over time, though, after it all starts to settle down enough for me to remember to breathe, some other stuff emerges as God works on my soul.

Way below the junk, there are these glimmers of trust. I am a child of God, and I love him. And somewhere in the deepest recesses of my soul, which are being exposed to the light from the cracks, I know he loves me.

There is a little girl inside who wants to grow a soul whose identity is in Christ. A soul that, when stripped of all else, remains intact and glowing because she knows she'll be okay in the hand of her Father. There is someone who knows that her impatience is really about a lack of trust in God, and she wants to trust, to let go of the rushing of herself and others. There is someone who knows that the meanness in her critical spirit is about fear and pride, and when she lets it go, she becomes a person she really likes, a person she longs to be.

And then we, God and I, can rebuild from the inside out . . . the best way to build.

CHAPTER 4

Before the First Rays

I arise in the morning torn between a desire to improve the world and a desire to enjoy the world. This makes it hard to plan the day.

ELWYN BROOKS WHITE

I WAS ON MY WAY TO MEET A FRIEND FOR A HIKE followed by lunch. The drive was glorious, winding through the brown velvet hills dotted with oak trees on a warm, sunny California morning. I knew that the next few hours would be filled with much of what I love most: being outdoors on a hot day, strenuous physical exertion, and good food and iced tea. All of it infused with the animated conversation of two friends who had gone past the expiration date on their need to catch up.

Just minutes before I pulled into the hiking area, three sharp beeps came over the radio. An AMBER Alert had been issued.

For the next sixty seconds a description of the person who had abducted a young girl was blasted across the airways. Then came the make, model, and color of the vehicle, along with a partial license plate number. Location of abduction. And finally a description of the six-year-old girl: hair color, eye color, and the mention of the pink shirt she wore with a cartoon figure on it.

And there I was . . . torn. While my next few hours would be full of joy, wonder, and connection, a mother and a father would be living on the edge of their life. I would be drinking in nonstop goodness; they would need to be medicated in order to take their next breaths.

That torn place is a hard place to be. So hard that almost every time we are there, we are in a rush to move beyond, to get to a spot that is not so divided. From time to time during our hike, conversation, and lunch, I thought of that little girl. I whispered prayers but could not shake the contrast of what I imagined was her terror and my joy, coexisting in these same hours.

In its most benign forms, living divided is awkward. When it's malignant, however, it tears at the very fabric of our souls. It's nearly impossible to reconcile the opposing sides. And I should probably rewrite that last sentence and leave out the word *nearly*.

That kind of living in the middle is excruciating and causes disequilibrium. The dissonance that is created when things are in such a state of conflict—when we go through experiences that are so opposite it is nearly impossible to resolve them—makes us go just a little bit crazy.

Social psychologists refer to this contrast as cognitive dissonance. They explain that our motivation to reduce dissonance is so strong that either we try to ignore or deny one reality, or we adjust our belief system to create one with consistency. And we do much of this at an unconscious level.

After hearing the AMBER Alert and feeling the sadness, I quickly thought, *Well, there's nothing I can do, and I sure don't want to ruin my hike and my time with Lisa.*

Part of that is right. The police were on it; the AMBER Alert was blaring; I didn't even know the girl's name. I really was incapable of helping in any way other than praying (and don't get me wrong, I believe deeply in the power of prayer, but if that were *my* kid? I'd want prayer *and* the police).

But part of that thinking is just to protect my comfort. I'd rather not have my enjoyment divided by the reality of someone else's devastating pain.

I think Jesus was torn when he wept over the mourners at Lazarus's funeral (see John 11:35); I think he was torn when he felt compassion on seeing his people harassed and helpless (see Matthew 9:36); I think the apostle Paul was torn when he wrote in Romans 7: "I do not do the good I want to do, but the evil I do not want to do—this I keep on doing" (verse 19). I think God was torn when he created this perfect Eden-earth for his people and they marred it, and he had to start all over again. I think we live torn.

My son and I had three days of skiing and snowboarding ahead of us. At the end of the first day, my son asked me to join him on a more difficult run than I had been skiing that day. He had been snowboarding on the upper runs, and I hadn't seen much of him except at lunch. I initially demurred, saying I wasn't sure I could handle that run, but Johnny assured me I could.

Caught between my accurate assessment of my skiing skills and my joy at being asked by my son to join him, I caved. All the way up on the chairlift, I kept thinking, *It'll be fine. It'll be the last run of the day anyway.*

Yup. It was.

Largely because my release gauge wasn't set properly, my skis failed to give way when I fell in the icy bowl at the top of the run. My body slid down the slope while my right leg, stuck in the ski, twisted and pulled in the opposite direction.

I made it to the bottom of the run and tried to ski down the rest of the way to the lodge (after all, I didn't see any blood). That didn't work, so I rode the chairlift down. By the time I was on the lift, my knee looked like a cantaloupe. By the time the MRI was finished, I was told I had completely torn my ACL and I'd broken both my femur and my tibia.

My orthopedic surgeon is a genius, and the work he did with a cadaver ligament corrected the damage done by the tear. I have complete function in that leg again, and I have skied numerous times since (hardly ever on a slope suggested by my son).

But I can still feel something inside my knee. It works great, for which I am incredibly grateful, but there is a sense inside that knee that makes me aware of the tear. It's not a big deal, but I can tell.

My grandmother wasn't one to dwell on difficulties of the past, so I have a vivid memory of one of the few times she talked about her husband's (my grandfather's) death. I was four at the time he died, and I have only wispy but sweet recollections of him. His death had been fairly sudden. He suffered a heart attack at the age of fifty-seven, and he was in the hospital less than a day when he passed away.

"It felt like my body got torn in half. Like someone had literally ripped away part of me." I remember her using the word *torn*, and it conjured up in me an image of her wounded body, ragged, exposed, raw, and bleeding. I had never heard someone describe anything like that before. She was a widow years before she thought possible. Her life partner was irretrievably gone. Life was never the same. It was a big deal.

Sometimes tears are so unthinkable that *torn* barely begins to describe the wrenching cataclysm. There is a family at our church—mom and dad, three teenage boys, and a dog. They live about eight blocks from us and have been quite involved in our church, he as an elder, she as a connector with a ministry in the Tenderloin section of San Francisco.

Almost two years ago, the dad, who was in his late fifties, was diagnosed with prostate cancer. Except they didn't catch it at an early stage. By the time the discomfort began and the blood tests came back, it was at stage four. His bones were riddled with it.

Treatments began and prayers ensued, but after about eighteen months of trying new protocols to stay ahead of it, the doctors delivered the news that they had nothing left to try. His blood count was low, his skin was white and cold, and the cancer was advancing. Time was limited—most likely less than a year.

And then their sixteen-year-old son took his life.

There needs to be space even on this page to begin to take that in.

There have been only a handful of times in my life when I have been in the presence of such a raw grief, the kind that was in their house that night. As you can imagine, there are all kinds of complexities to this story—I'm sure more than I even know. The ones I do know . . . well, that's their story to tell, not mine.

What is on this page is enough to turn our faces toward a kind of grief that tears at our hearts, minds, souls, and bodies. Darkness. Anguish and misery and clutching. Tears, shock, disbelief.

And faith.

Little strands of it, strong enough in certain moments to stand against the pain and hold them, to tether them, to each other and to God. Words were uttered aloud to each other, in between chokes and sobs, that provided a thin ray of light.

Who knows where it will all go from here? It is too soon to tell.

The ups and downs to come are nearly impossible to imagine. Right now there are people and meals, phone calls and flowers. There are errands and listening ears. We are holding their hands, caught somewhere between our desperate hurt for them and our deep fear of that kind of precariousness in life. The funeral was amazing, overwhelming almost. Nearly two thousand people spilled out the doors of our church, many of them teenagers from the school their boys attend.

But soon, and necessarily, the calls will thin out and the visits will be fewer. At the end of the day, people have to go back to their lives, and this family to theirs. No one can go through grief on behalf of another.

Support is wonderful—a lifeline, really. But there is always space between us, even when our fingers are touching, and that space is where they will have to live.

Not only will the support subside from the level it is now, but life will ensue. The cable company will make a mistake on their billing; the dog will ingest something and need to go to the vet. They will be swallowed up in the tide of life surging forward into the future, with its mundane circumstances along with its wonder and magic.

And they will be caught between. There is a tear there so deep I cannot imagine what will fall into that gulf. Doubt, anger, depression, begging, numbness, and surging and searing pain.

We and others will be there for them over the long haul,

in whatever ways we can. But that is wholly inadequate. God will need to be there, or they are lost.

When pain is this fresh and this awful, I'm not sure much light can get through. You have to wait for some of the initial jolt to subside, to let something settle enough that you can emerge from being stunned before you can look for a ray of light. And waiting is excruciating when you are torn.

CHAPTER 5

A Box Full of Darkness

Someone I loved once gave me a box full of darkness.
It took me years to understand that this, too, was a gift.

MARY OLIVER

WE HAD BEEN IN THE DOMINICAN REPUBLIC for just over a week. The team from our church, including my then thirteen-year-old daughter, Laura, had been mixing concrete, tying rebar, and laying concrete bricks for a new wing of the school we were serving. During our breaks, we would often join the children at recess and play games.

The island was tropical and warm, with banana and rubber trees swaying next to the palms. Nearly everything we saw or did reminded us that we were in another land. Each evening some of the folks from the school would add charcoal to the large outdoor grills, handmade out of rusted steel barrels. The chicken, marinated in something I'm pretty sure we'll have in heaven, was plated next to rice and fruit, and we spent most of the evenings eating, talking, singing, and laughing.

Cold showers cleaned off the day's grime after hard work in the intense sun. The challenge then was to fall asleep, lying on top of sleeping bags on hard bunk beds. In the morning, the roosters and the early sun would start the day again. Each day was marked by long hours of physical labor as we worked alongside and under the direction of the local Dominicans, who were deeply invested in expanding this school in one of the poorest neighborhoods in the city.

Toward the end of our time there, our hosts took a few of us who were interested to visit the medical clinic. It was a small concrete building with a few rooms that housed rudimentary medical equipment. As a former RN, I marveled at how much good they got done with so little.

There was a sweet bustle of activity in the clinic that day, with many children waiting with a parent, and a handful of elderly patients. Some of the outward signs of the health issues were startling: twisted and useless limbs, skin markings that indicated systemic disease, and emaciation that made me avert my eyes. More reminders that we were in another land indeed.

As we were finishing our tour, we passed by a room that had photos of a wide variety of people, from teens to the elderly—all of them with wide grins on their faces. It seemed to be an exam room. Then someone told me that this was their cataract room. I was intrigued.

It seems that a handful of years prior, a doctor who worked

in the clinic went through training in the United States to learn a cataract surgery procedure. He was sent for the training to help address this significant need in the community. Since the sun on the island is so intense, and since so many of the people had outdoor jobs such as farming, the incidence of vision loss from cataracts was quite high.

Almost imperceptibly, over time, these people would fall victim to the damaging rays. Their lenses would react by becoming more and more opaque, and eventually whatever sight they had was reduced to a small field of mostly blur.

Now that there was someone in the village who could perform a corrective procedure, it was like small miracles were happening in that clinic.

Imagine uneducated, poor, rural islanders who found the time to travel to this clinic to try to understand why their vision was fading. They knew that, unchecked, this condition would surely lead to their being incapacitated, helpless, and unable to make even a small living. They would walk into the clinic with cloudy vision, as if someone had smeared Vaseline over their eyes, and they'd emerge with twenty-twenty vision. The procedure removed the cloudy lens and let the light back in.

What we were seeing that day was the result of years of work, however. Apparently when the clinic had first opened, they had very few takers. They had a difficult time identifying the cataract sufferers and persuading them to come to the clinic. So what turned the tide? When a handful of people who'd had the surgery went out into the rural parts of the island and told their stories.

These storytellers were cataract sufferers who'd had their sight restored. They were so overwhelmed with joy and gratitude that any residue of shame that had once followed them fell away. And their story could not be contained. They *had* to tell it, they *had* to find others like them who needed to hear it, to believe it.

These folks who had suffered with cataracts for years could recognize fellow sufferers. The recently healed natives noticed the slight angle that those who still suffered held their heads at as they squinted their eyes, straining to see what used to be clear. The storytellers would introduce themselves, describe the slow loss of vision, and tell how a simple procedure could change all that.

Once these former patients became storytellers in the villages, cataract sufferers from all over the island began lining up at the clinic. They went from treating one or two patients a month to needing an appointment system to handle the large number of people who were coming to have their vision restored.

There it is . . . again. The power of a story: from brokenness to wholeness. And it did what other things had not been able to do. A glossy brochure. A health class taught in the towns. Rather, it was one person telling another, "I was blind, but now I see. And here's where you can go to have that same experience."

It's not just a story. For those who hear the story—when they are in the same kind of pain—that story becomes life. It might be a nice story up to that point, or mildly interesting.

But when that story is personal, it becomes enthralling and necessary. The listeners hang on every word, hoping against hope it might be true for them, too.

Stories are powerful, but stories from brokenness, stories that intersect with another's pain—that, my friend, is life-changing stuff. This is gospel. Good news. Great news, really. It is the same power that puts us in the fight for justice, for serving the poor and the marginalized in the name of Jesus. It's what keeps us, in the face of overwhelming odds, going the other direction, using hope as the shield for the fight against human trafficking, poverty, and inequitable access to health care, education, and work.

In the first chapter of 2 Corinthians, Paul opens with a simple but deep reminder: "God . . . the Father of compassion and the God of all comfort . . . comforts us in all our troubles, so that we can comfort those in any trouble with the comfort we ourselves receive from God. For just as we share abundantly in the sufferings of Christ, so also our comfort abounds through Christ" (verses 3-5).

It is in our suffering, in our brokenness, in our troubles, that God invades our lives. In those times, both the sufferings and the comfort of Jesus can take root.

God, who is the source of all compassion, felt that compassion so deeply that he was willing to go with the idea of sending his Son to be the ultimate compassion for us. In this way, he moved to offer us comfort, to offer us consolation and freedom from pain.

Sounds pretty amazing, right?

I don't know. See, I like a good story as much as the next person. In fact, I love getting caught up in a good telling of a dramatic turn of events or help that came when someone couldn't see it coming. I really like stories of other people's brokenness and how they experienced the depths of God in them. It's my own story of brokenness that I don't like. Don't like and really don't want you to know about. And I don't think I'm the only one.

Our walls are up; our faces are painted. We smile, we nod, and we talk about *pleasant things*. We want the light to come in, at least theoretically. But we'd like it to come in while we're smiling. We don't like that the cracks have to appear in order for the light to get in.

Seriously, there's just got to be a better way. We could buy the light, borrow it. Pretend we have it. But to have to be broken to get it? Hmm, maybe not.

I think I'd rather stay in the dark about my darkness. I could pretend it's not dark or, better yet, convince myself my darkness isn't as dark as others' darkness. Nope, I'm pretty sure it's not. So even though my toes are stubbed and my arms are bruised from knocking into things I couldn't see, my denial is tougher. And more comfortable, thank you very much.

On the afternoon we were at the Dominican cataract clinic, the doctor invited me into the exam room since I had some background in health care. A man who had undergone his surgery fourteen days prior was there for a checkup. He looked much older than his years, thanks to a combination of the harsh tropical sun and backbreaking outdoor work. His skin was leathered and his grin nearly toothless.

The doctor unwrapped the bandage from around his eyes. He then finished his exam and declared the patient to be healing and on the way to complete health. "It all looks good. By the end of next week, you can stop using the eye drops I gave you."

The man just sat there. His head began to move from side to side, and one big tear from each eye slid down the furrows of his face.

He clutched the doctor's arm and said something in a low voice, over and over. My basic Spanish skills recognized the words: "I can see, I can see, I can see." Then there was an outpouring of "Gracias" that lasted another minute.

The vision loss had come on so slowly that he'd hardly noticed how bad it was. After a while, he couldn't imagine there was anything to be done about it. Then he heard someone tell him his story. His eyes too, had been broken. But there was a place—others could go there too.

It's easy to think that darkness is just in the dramatic things—blind eyes, the death of a child, a tragic diagnosis. But darkness is everywhere. So is light. And darkness in any of its forms needs light.

I had planned a fun day with Laura when she was twelve years old—a "kidnap day," we called it. I got the idea from my brother-in-law after I'd been on one too many field trips, breathing in exhaust fumes on an old school bus, assigned to a group of kids that did not include my kid, and returning home feeling like I'd never want to repeat that experience again. Craig invented the idea of a kidnap day with his kids. Once a year, after dropping them off at school, he would reappear about thirty minutes later at the office, requesting that his child be called out of class for the rest of the day.

Today was Laura's day, and following the initial thrill of pulling her out of school, we embarked on a day to remember. I had lots of great things planned, and by midafternoon we found ourselves rushing to the ticket line to buy tickets for a movie. We were running a bit late, and I didn't want to miss the start of the film.

The guy in the ticket booth could not have been any slower. He was taking his time, and then he couldn't seem to get the ticket selection correct. Did I mention I was in a hurry?

I was rude. Not horribly, just sneakily. You know— speaking in clipped tones, repeating myself with an attitude, whisking the tickets out of his hand the moment he attempted to hand them to me. No words, just subtext meant to communicate disdain.

I acted with the kind of darkness that is so under the surface I was sure Laura wouldn't even notice. About five minutes into the film, she leaned over to whisper to me. Knowing my sweet, tenderhearted daughter, I readied myself for a cozy "Mom, this is the best day ever!"

"Mom, I think you were rude to that guy who gave us our tickets."

It's amazing how many disparate factors your brain can

handle at one time. I was hearing what I didn't expect, I was hearing what I didn't want to hear, and I was realizing that there was nothing in what she said that wasn't true. Close on the heels of all of that processing was the rapidly forming and about-to-emerge thought: *Not really, honey. He wasn't doing his job well, and we were about to miss the movie.*

Fortunately (and painfully), somewhere between what I heard and what I was about to say, the Holy Spirit intervened— sort of wedged himself between those two points in time and suggested that before I respond, I might want to consider first.

"Laura, you're right. I am *so* sorry. I was a jerk to him, and I'm embarrassed. When the movie is finished, I need to apologize to him."

That seemed to satisfy Laura, but it made it just a tad difficult for me to engage in the movie, knowing that each minute the plot progressed was bringing me closer to an awkward conversation with someone I didn't even know.

The credits rolled, the houselights came up, and Laura and I headed for the lobby. The guy was still behind the ticket counter. "Excuse me," I said. "I need to apologize for the way I spoke to you when I purchased our tickets."

He was a gangly teenage boy with bad skin and worse eye contact. "No, really, that's okay," he muttered.

"It's really not okay. I was rude, and I'm sorry."

"It's okay."

I was clearly not getting through. I think he was hoping I would go away. (I need to tell you at this point that I was hoping his shift would have been over before the movie ended.)

"Please, pay attention to me for a minute. I was a b----, and I need to apologize to you. Will you accept my apology?"

His eyes widened, and his face softened. Then he smiled a bit and nodded his head. A little light got in. It wasn't a cataract-causing blindness, but I had damaged him. Deep inside where no one else could see it. And maybe a little on the outside, where Laura could see it as well. I wish I had never acted that way in the first place. I wish I'd had appropriate patience with him, seeing as it was *my* lateness that meant we might miss the start of the movie.

But I did act that way. And who knows, it's quite possible that the way I treated that boy was just one more in a long line of incidents when people treated him like that. Incidents that were piling up in the hidden parts of his soul, eroding it a bit, tearing it and breaking it.

Remarkably, when I apologized and made him pay attention, the light didn't just invade his soul. It flooded mine.

CHAPTER 6

Dark Night of the Soul

*The most beautiful people we have known are those who
have known defeat, known suffering, known struggle, known
loss, and have found their way out of the depths. These persons
have an appreciation, a sensitivity, and an understanding of
life that fills them with compassion, gentleness, and a deep
loving concern. Beautiful people do not just happen.*

ELISABETH KÜBLER-ROSS

NERVE ENDINGS HAVE A PURPOSE. When activated by pain,
they unapologetically send an urgent message: "Move away!"
The nerve pathways from the skin to the brain operate at
warp speed, making the lapse between touching something
sharp or hot and recoiling an imperceptible period of time.

There isn't time for the brain to go through a deliber-
ate decision-making process. There isn't time to engage the
cerebral cortex in its best higher-level thinking. It's time for a
preprogrammed response that is immediate and also includes
"Don't return to this!" Such a reaction not only protects us
but also teaches us to avoid what hurts us.

Therein lies the rub: pain prevention is a great system for

avoiding bleeding and death . . . but maybe it's not so great for shaping a soul.

Some of the deepest and most effective soul work emerges from living in our wounds (not wallowing in them), probing and exploring them (again, not wallowing in them), and surrendering to God in them (not being a martyr). This is seriously counterintuitive work for a brain that works so hard to protect us. The system that works so well for us when we cut our fingers may not serve us so well when our hearts are pierced.

The patient in Room 310 had an injury to his ankle that had shattered many of the bones, and the surgical repair took hours, patience, a steady hand, and lots of steel. The surgeon had to stabilize the joint with rods and pins that were sunk deep into the patient's bone and emerged through the surface of his skin. As one of his nurses, I was responsible for keeping his incision clean and the antibiotics flowing to prevent infection from setting into the bone.

Despite meticulous care, just a week after the surgery, that is exactly what happened. When the wound exposed the tissue and bones to the air, it created a perfect opportunity for bacteria to cultivate. And it did.

The patient was in that room for eight months. More than two hundred and forty days. In isolation, with limited visitors. Medical personnel had to put on gowns, gloves, and masks just to enter the room and have a conversation. We were in there multiple times a day, cleaning the affected area, bandaging the wound, and administering medication. It was slow and agonizing. There were days when it didn't look like it was going to heal. There was even talk of amputation.

The healing process had to be from the inside out, or the wound would simply rupture open and we would have to start all over again.

But ever so slowly, hope grew faster than the bacteria did behind the door of that hospital room. There was healing that started deep within, and it eventually made its way to the surface.

The day the patient was cleared to go home, we had a party. We decorated the hallway he would be wheeled out through. We applauded for him and for his family, who had endured so much for so long to get him well.

In the weeks that followed, it was strange seeing new patients in Room 310. He had been in there for such a long time.

Wounds are like that. They take a long time to heal, especially if you want them to heal all the way through. And when something already hurts, if we hear it's also going to take a long time to get better . . . well, it's no wonder we avoid going there.

We are all wounded and broken people. Sometimes it takes getting wounded to remember that. And then when we are in pain, it takes a long time to settle down and face it.

I was facing a devastating situation that was external to me while at the same time I was on an inward journey to face some dark, internal corners of my soul. Once again, I had no concept yet of the connection. One of my kids had been on a slow drift, years in the making. And now it was clear. The distance and the choices were painful and confusing. No resolution was on the horizon. I felt the kind of searing, disorienting pain that only comes when your child is involved. At one point during all of this, I found myself with a free weekend. Everyone in the house except my son was gone.

Johnny, not fully aware of what I was going through, suggested we take an overnight trip up north, along the coast. I was grateful for the companionship and the retreat. Almost as soon as our car pulled out of the driveway, I felt a slight release in my heart and a drop in the anxiety as I escaped for a short time, the space creating a much-needed margin for my pain.

The next twenty-four hours were spent reveling in the scenery, exchanging fun bursts of conversations with my son, eating good meals, and watching a movie that involved zombies and blood. I never forgot my pain, but there was a respite in all of this that eased it, if only for a bit.

When it was time for us to head home, almost as soon as we turned the car south, I could feel everything returning. I dreaded going back to the world where there was no respite. About halfway home, Johnny suggested that we stop at a picturesque place where the Russian River empties into the sea amid a redwood forest. He was anxious to get in a surfing session before lunch, and I was glad for the chance to walk along the beach before we got back into the car for our final leg home.

Not long after we stopped, I stepped barefoot onto the beach, bundled up against the wind and the clouds, and carrying my sadness. Just then a busload of high school kids from a local church spilled out onto the beach. They were high on Jesus, laughing and tracing words along the shore. I didn't pay much attention to them until I turned to walk back to the car and saw what one group had carved into the sand:

The Lord is my shepherd, I shall not want.

I walked by the words slowly, taking them in as I passed.

Strangely, my first response was to view myself from above, imagining this brokenhearted woman (me) seeing those words and being deeply moved and comforted in her pain. A serendipitous intersection of the truth of God and my anguish—a beautiful resolution.

But . . .

My second response was very different, very visceral, and very immediate. I said out loud (to God) but not loud enough for anyone else to hear, "You are a shepherd? I would imagine a good shepherd would take care of his sheep. Do you have any idea how much pain I'm in? You're not a shepherd. Not even close."

I mumbled it just loud enough for me to hear, over and over, up and down the beach. It felt good to say. I savored every word.

It's funny what the pain from a wound can unlock. It felt like the anguish was coming from a deep and unknown place inside me. It was more than overwhelming—it seemed as though it would consume me. Like a wounded animal—cornered, hurt, and panicked—I lashed out at God.

I haven't had many "dark night of the soul" experiences, but I've had enough. Previous to that season, I'd gone through times that were excruciating, and in them God had excavated my soul. So I questioned if I'd really learned anything during those previous times for me to have such a raw response to God on this one. But I knew he'd been doing something inside me. I knew that I'd been dragged deep into the recesses of my soul and that spiritual surgery had been done.

And now here was another tough time, and God was inviting me deeper. That's not where I wanted to go, but having been wounded before, I knew that was where I needed to go. At some level, I knew that's where healing is found.

And like with a wounded animal, God let me spin and rail, cry and rage, avoid and withdraw, and ache. Just kind of wear myself out.

An older man at our church—eighty-six, to be exact—had become a good friend. When he spoke about his past, the wounds seemed fresh and tender. As I listened to his stories, I wasn't sure which had inflicted more pain: the years of physical abuse, which had left him with scars, or the verbal abuse, which left scars that were less visible.

One day he opened up to me about something long buried.

It was a tender moment, a kind of gift. Certainly there had been healing over the years, in different ways and to differing degrees. But the pain wasn't just a scar; it was still a wound. As he kept talking, it was clear that this wound kept him returning to God for further healing—to share the pain, the emptiness, the parts of his life that had been irretrievably affected by this broken relationship.

After some time, the sparkle began to return to his eyes. He was grateful that the wound served as a kind of fetter, keeping him in God's orbit. He was, he said, more grateful for Jesus at age eighty-six than he had ever been. As he said that, I could hardly breathe—just for a moment, but unmistakably. It was, for me, a holy moment. It made me rethink my own wounds. It made me want to be more grateful for Jesus when I'm eighty-six. (If.)

When I asked him what allowed him to take his wounds to God, he chuckled.

"Well, for a long time, I didn't. But after I'd tried just about everything else to cover them, soothe them, or explain them, I realized that they had impacted almost everything in me. And where else was there left to go but to God? I thought I'd give that a try."

And there he sat, across the table from me, with a face wrinkled by the years and eyes that reflected a spirit that had not dimmed. It made me wonder if wounds might be some kind of beauty treatment.

I have a friend who has recently gone through some tough stuff—not life threatening or anything, just really hard. It mostly involved a working relationship with someone who was very difficult, and the conflict-avoidance cycle was maddening. She thought those wounds had completely healed, but it turned out they'd just been covered over. Nerves were touched, and pain was rife.

During this time, my friend was truly introduced to her stuff. She met her avoidance, her pride, her abdication, and her shame. This difficult person and this difficult situation and all her stuff—well, they all collided. So she picked up the pieces and brought them to God.

Just a few days ago, I talked to her on the phone. All of this—the work God was doing in and with her—she called "brutal and beautiful."

I have been thinking about that phrase ever since.

Brutal and beautiful.

Like scars that tell a story.

Come, let us return to the LORD.
He has torn us to pieces
    but he will heal us;
he has injured us
    but he will bind up our wounds.
After two days he will revive us;
    on the third day he will restore us,
    that we may live in his presence.

HOSEA 6:1-2

I underlined these verses when I was in graduate school and going through another difficult time. I hadn't noticed them before. That's another wonderful thing wounds have to offer us. They cause us to pay attention to the right things; they open us up to truths and to those truths working in us in a fresh way. Desperation is a powerful clarifier and motivator.

Our wounds; God's healing. Our injuries; God's binding.

And if we allow God to touch us in our pain, he won't just put a Band-Aid over the gaping wound; he will see that we get healed from the inside out. He revives and restores us, and then, as Hosea says in verse 3, we are drawn to acknowledge him.

Let us acknowledge the LORD;
> let us press on to acknowledge him.
As surely as the sun rises,
> he will appear;
he will come to us like the winter rains,
> like the spring rains that water the earth.

I don't think it's a coincidence that the word *acknowledge* is used twice in that one verse. It's not enough for us to see our wounds and then be healed. A response is required of us.

We are wounded; God heals; we acknowledge him.

Don't be fooled by the simplicity.

CHAPTER 7

The Paradox of Darkness

When I looked for God in the light, God was not there. When I faced the unfaceable, I found that I had joined God in the darkness. And so, paradoxically, the darkness had become light.

AVERY BROOKE

DARKNESS COMES IN ALL SHADES. Sudden blindness, creeping cataracts. Twenty years ago, when I was a young mom (our kids were nine, seven, and five), we moved to Chicago. I had been through life events in the past that were much higher on the Richter scale, but in this case it was the gradual darkness that caught me by surprise.

For me, the losses from this move, while not at the deepest levels of life and death, were on multiple levels. We were moving primarily for my husband's work, and I felt a bit lost in that. My kids were experiencing varying degrees of pain or joy over the move, and as a mom, I carried their pain in a deep part of my heart.

I am a California girl, through and through. If there is some sort of DNA that might define that, I have no doubt my genes carry that strand. The texture and topography of the land, the hills that push up into mountains, the sea that is always at hand. The steady sun. The vibrant flowers that bloom year round.

Chicago? Not so much—none of that. I know it doesn't sound like much in the grand scheme of difficulties, but you don't get to decide the grand scheme of difficulty for someone else. So Chicago? Really tough for me.

No sun—hardly ever any sun. The place makes Seattle seem like Florida.

No job—I had left that behind.

And the friends I'd had from the time I was born were now three thousand miles away.

It wasn't a death or a life-threatening illness, I will give you that. But I think that's part of why it hit me in such a surprising way. It was a series of minor losses that, when combined, felt like a nuclear wallop.

The first few weeks were a whirl of activity. We had to stay in a La Quinta hotel for nearly a week since the house was in the final days of escrow. Getting three elementary-school kids ready in a hotel bathroom, eating breakfast at the buffet bar (my kids still fondly recall the all-you-can-eat bacon at that place), and dropping them off at a new school. Meeting the moving van after a week and starting the endless process of unpacking boxes and turning a house into a home. Not to mention trying to find a comforting stuffed animal or a missing backpack in all those boxes. New dentist and doctors, new grocery store aisles, no job, no friends. And then the snow started.

Part of it was a grand adventure, so I didn't see the shadow sneaking up on me. We had been there about two months when I crawled into bed one night and said to John, "I can't find God here." That started a long conversation about what that meant and what we should do about it. I knew, or thought I knew, that God really was in Chicago (although I wouldn't have blamed him if he wasn't), but I didn't *really* know it. It wasn't in my reality.

John, wanting to help, jumped in, saying, "Well, maybe we shouldn't have moved here and we should go back." At least, at the time I thought he was trying to help. Later he admitted he mostly said it to guilt me into not feeling that way. So much to learn in marriage, right?

I didn't know much, but one thing I did know. Moving back would not solve this. Only living in the reality of it (did I mention I didn't buy a winter coat until the end of our second year living in Chicago?) and waiting, straining, fighting, and waiting some more to find God. I might not be smart, but I am scrappy.

And I knew somewhere deep down that *through* was the only way forward.

When we first arrived in Chicago, after the initial weeks of flurry to get settled gave way to a new normalcy, the darkness descended. I felt an underlying and chronic sadness that was so different from my normal personality. Nothing seemed like light, and it was hard to see my way forward.

In the large scope of things, this wasn't even a monumental issue. While a geographical move is certainly capable of shaking the foundation of your world and therefore your soul, it's a drop in the bucket of world-altering shifts that leave you groping for God, who seemed so close just a minute ago.

Over the next year, ever so gradually, the light began to widen, and the darkness dissipated. God *was* in Chicago. My kids adjusted and thrived, and I found a job that may be among the best I've ever had. Friends emerged, including relationships that continue to this day. And every once in a while, I saw the sun.

Now, ten years after landing back in California (where I intend to live until I die), I go back to visit Chicago sometimes, mostly for work. I have fond memories of that time and of how my soul grew roots in that frigid soil. Roots that ache when I drive past our old house or the school the kids attended. Things inside my soul that I didn't know even needed healing were touched during that season. My understanding of who God is grew exponentially.

You could have told me that at the time, like I am telling you. But it wouldn't have helped. Transformation is an inside job.

There are certain defining points in history—times when darkness was all there was. A kind of darkness the world has rarely seen, an unthinkable darkness. Looking backward, we imagine, *What would I have done?* And from the vantage point of the future, we can look for those minuscule flashes of light that led people out of the suffocating void.

The year was 1938. In the years following World War I, a growing movement took root in Germany, sparked in part by the humiliation of the Treaty of Versailles. As early as 1920, the Nazi party was touting an ideology of national superiority and anti-Semitism. In 1935, the Nuremberg Laws were passed, which initiated the exclusion of Jews and eventually enforced their migration into crowded ghetto regions of major cities.

November 9, 1938, about a year before the official start of the Second World War, marked the "night of shattered glass." *Kristallnacht.* On a shadowy night that ushered in deep darkness, the windows of Jewish-owned stores, homes, schools, hospitals, and synagogues were smashed throughout Germany and Austria.

In a single night of terror, German soldiers ransacked buildings, demolished property with sledgehammers, forced people from their homes, torched buildings, and beat people who had awoken to this confusion. Largely seen now as the beginning of the Holocaust, this night initiated the systematic genocide of Jews. They were eventually moved into slave and extermination camps, and by the time the war was over, six million had died from exhaustion, disease, and gas chambers.

For six million people, the light went out. The darkness was great. The world was not watching, and no one was coming to help.

As the darkness intensified, in a small farming village in south-central France, a thin ray of light forced its way through. The Protestant villagers in Le Chambon-sur-Lignon had a history of facing the darkness themselves. As the first Protestants in an exclusively Catholic country, the Huguenots knew what it was to be persecuted. Over the past several hundred years, they had endured religious oppression in the form of confiscation of property, lifelong imprisonment, and even death—including being burned at the stake.

This was their history. It was a deep part of who they were. These were the stories they told late at night to the next generation, stories that had dramatically shaped their hearts and souls. Stories from the 1500s to the 1700s that had made them who they were in 1942.

And who they were in 1942 was nothing but light.

Word spread that there was a place in France that was taking in Jewish refugees. As it became clear that the German "relocation" plans really meant death, many Jews began frantically searching for escape. Over the course of four years, until the end of the war, around five thousand people were sheltered in this village, often to the peril of those who sheltered them.

Several decades after the war ended, a film crew arrived in the village to interview those who had hidden Jews. They wanted to be sure this story was told before the "saints of light" had passed.

As the world looked back on the horror that was the Holocaust, they called what happened in Le Chambon "a conspiracy of goodness" and "moral consensus on a grand scale." The world was amazed, humbled, and inspired . . . and people could not help but ask themselves, "What would I have done?"

As the cameras rolled, folks like local minister André Trocmé and housewife Emma Héritier told the story. Of how the people came; of how the villagers opened their homes, their basements, their barns, the forest. No one was turned away.

Sometimes, they said, when German soldiers would arrive looking for evidence supporting the rumors that were flying about Jewish refugees in the area, the villagers would move the Jewish people into the forest. There they would wait while the Germans conducted an invasive search of homes and places of business.

When the search proved fruitless, they would leave, and a handful of the villagers would go to the edge of the forest and sing a predetermined song—a song that indicated it was safe to come out of the forest.

Toward the end of the film, when the remarkable story had been told, the inevitable question was posed to the aging villagers: "Were you afraid?"

Throughout the telling of the story, there had been pauses after the questions as the interviewees thought, remembered, and considered. But this time the answer was immediate.

"No. We were used to it."

No? Really? How could that answer roll so quickly from their tongues, with no hesitation at all?

We were used to it. These Huguenots, descended from a people who had been oppressed for hundreds of years, had persecution in their blood. They remembered their own history, and their response to the persecution of another persecuted group (the scope of which no one could have even imagined at the time) mattered to them. And the choice—more than easy—was reflexive.

Over time, the darkness that for hundreds of years had threatened to overtake them and snuff them out became a kind of light. Sometimes darkness can do that. It brings us to the bedrock of our souls, and depending on what we find there, it can lead us out of despair and into hope. And that hope is strong—a tensile filament that is not easily broken, that conducts and emits a powerful light. That's the kind of light that can emerge from darkness.

Because here's what darkness does. It forces us to face fears, silence, and pain. It insists on hard questions of meaning, purpose, and significance. It strips us of the superficial and asks if that absence leaves a vacuum or something of more substance. We fight in the darkness because the return to the superficial would be so much easier, but wholly without comfort. We fight in the darkness because we are afraid we have no answers—or we do have the answers but they are not to our liking. We fight in the darkness, but like Jacob, it is in the fighting that God touches us.

Sometimes the descent into the darkness is necessary. We live too easily on the surface; it is pleasant there, warm and comfortable. But there are haunting questions. As I watch this film about the French village of salvation, I want to be like those villagers I saw interviewed. I imagine my noble self answering with the same ease they answered with. I see myself a hero, just like they are, in a movie.

But this isn't a movie. It's a film about a real time, with real people who took life-defying risks for others, with nothing in it for themselves except the pleasure of acting out of the deepest parts of their souls—the parts that were forged over hundreds of years, on the backs of their parents and grandparents and great-great-greats.

That kind of strength doesn't come from a wish to be a certain kind of person. It comes from the darkness, from living there long enough to see the light—a thin sliver at first, but light nonetheless. And realizing that the light is God. And that God, who has been there in the darkness all along, is stronger than any darkness that ever was.

That kind of experience shifts the pieces of our souls and reconstructs them until we become people who say *yes* without a second thought. Yes to helping when it inconveniences us, when it threatens us, when it taxes us. Yes to solidarity with others in their pain, when our lives may be just fine. This is the yes of the gospel.

Sometimes, when my life has been at its darkest—just a handful of times—I think about this. In the darkness, my strong instinct is to flee. Or at the very least, to do something to distract or numb me from what the darkness is forcing me to feel. But how does God shape a soul? Sometimes through the darkness. Sometimes the way to is through, and avoiding the darkness won't get us there. We have to live in it, knowing, hoping, there will be light.

In some of the worst times of my life, some of them lasting a few days, others months or years, it takes me a long time to surrender to what the darkness has for me. I fight and wrestle; I avoid and deny. There is a *lot* of swirling before there is quiet in me. On paper I believe that God is at the bottom of the darkness. That there is no darkness strong enough that even a slice of light from him can't overcome it. On paper I believe that.

The problem is that I don't live my life on paper, and very quickly as I enter the shadows that precede the darkness, I writhe to be released. I want a quick answer and an easy out—all before lunch, please. But that doesn't shape a soul. Or perhaps it's more accurate to say it does, just not in great ways.

So in the darkness, I sometimes push myself to think. About the eleven-year-old Jewish schoolgirl who was awakened in the middle of the night to shouts and the sounds of shattered glass. I think about her peering out the window to see her school being burned and some of her classmates being pulled out into the cold night to an awaiting deportation bus.

I think about the disbelief that rose in her when, over the ensuing months, it became clear that *Kristallnacht* was not just an isolated event but a slow-moving tsunami of horror overtaking everyone she knew and loved. I think about the possibility that she, during years in a concentration camp, made friends and played games, all the while being forced to work all day with little food or water. I think about what she might have experienced each night before she fell asleep in that dirty, rodent-infested room while nighttime stories of hope were told, only to awaken to find that someone else had died during the night.

I think about how the global reality of the Holocaust was a million stories of people like her, people who not only lived through it but clung to hope. Clung to something that was at the bottom of all of that overwhelming and unthinkable darkness.

And when I think of that, it helps me to sit still in my darkness. And wait. For God. Initially in the darkness, I think, *I can't find God here.* Eventually, though, I realize, *Oh yes, I can.* In fact, when I stay still enough to allow my eyes to adjust, I can see him most clearly of all.

Fifty-one years after the night of broken glass, the Berlin Wall came down. Fifty-one years to the night: November 9, 1989. Twenty-eight miles of stone fortress that had been created to separate, exclude, and kill—torn down, crumbled under the weight of hope and light.

During those fifty-one years, to be sure, the light was much smaller than the darkness. That is often the case. But clearly, smaller did not mean lesser or weaker. In fact, the power that was within the smaller made it all the more impressive when it managed to defeat the darkness.

I—we—sit at the feet of those who have lived in the darkness. Most of them, too, had periods of resistance, or at least wishing it weren't that way. But they stayed. And the way they emerged on the other side of the darkness contained so much light that we are torn between needing to look at them and needing to look away. Noble, stirring, courageous, lovely—the way a soul should look, but we forget it can and what it takes.

"My God, why have you forsaken me?" (Matthew 27:46). On the cross, Jesus despaired over where the light had gone. The light he was so familiar with. The light that was in him, the light that *was* him.

But three days later came his resurrection. A light that the world had never before seen, the strongest light that will ever be. And hundreds of years later, the light that burned in the hearts of those French Huguenots is still burning.

That kind of light, the light that shines in some of the darkest darkness the world has ever known, became a beacon, drawing thousands of threatened people to its side. A beacon declaring refuge and safety, even at great cost. An easy yes. Because that's the kind of light that can be bred in darkness. Strong, courageous, defiant. Light refined over hundreds of years. Light that sang a song at the edge of the forest. Olly olly oxen free.

CHAPTER 8

Awakening

*There is in us an instinct for newness, for renewal, for a
liberation of creative power. We seek to awaken in ourselves
a force which really changes our lives from within.*

THOMAS MERTON

GROWING UP IN THE MEDITERRANEAN CLIMATE of Southern California, I had few encounters with dormancy. The exception was in third grade, when my class captured a fuzzy black caterpillar in a jar with holes poked in the lid. To furnish the jar, we included leaves, some drops of water, and a stick for him to crawl on. At least we assumed it was a "he"—I have no idea why.

We watched that jar, day after day, as the busy caterpillar, moving like a Slinky, made his way up and down the twig, munching on leaves and seemingly content. After a while, our fuzzy friend began spinning his chrysalis, and over time, he completely entombed himself. You've seen this movie before, so you know how it ends, but for a bunch of eight-year-olds, this was all new. Giving him up for dead, we could hardly imagine what would happen when the teacher told us, "Just wait."

We were third graders—for us, waiting was that excruciating time between when the teacher told us recess was coming and when the bell actually rang, releasing us to that glorious playground. Waiting for several *weeks*? Are you kidding? Nah, we gave him up for dead.

Days went by, and our attention wandered from the jar to other things. We mostly forgot about our little caterpillar. When you're a kid, you're looking for immediate results, and a chrysalis just doesn't provide that. No, there was kickball and jump rope, red rover and the jungle gym. We played marbles, listened to Mrs. Lambright read us stories in class, and struggled to move our writing from printing to cursive, following the white letters outlined on the green colored posters that framed the chalkboard.

Then, weeks later, David Coleman walked by the jar and stopped. He bent over and watched for a few minutes before he shrieked, "It's moving!"

Judging by the class's reaction, he might as well have cried out, "It's a three-headed kitten!"

All thirty-four of us crowded around him, pushing and saying, "Lemme see, lemme see!"

Sure enough, that brown chrysalis, which had spent the past few weeks looking like a dead leaf, was trembling. After the noise settled down, Mrs. Lambright told us that when we arrived at school the next morning, something remarkable was going to happen.

I've gotta tell you, from the perspective of an eight-year-old, she might as well have said, "When you turn thirty . . ."

The idea of having to go home, eat a snack, play, do homework, eat dinner, take a bath, watch TV, sleep (yeah, like *that* was going to happen), and then go through breakfast, brushing my teeth, getting dressed, and riding the bus to school before I could see what would happen next sounded like torture. Bring in Jack Bauer and slip the bamboo shoots under my fingernails—I'd take anything but having to wait until the morning! But Mrs. Lambright patiently explained that there was nothing we could do to speed up the process.

I thought I was simply waiting to meet a butterfly. Little did I know that seeds were being planted in my small brain and heart. Seeds of wonder, patience, hope, exuberance, patience, and patience.

On the way home that afternoon, in the third-grade section of the bus, all the buzz was about the chrysalis. We were sitting next to the first and second graders, and we were proud of our conversation, which these immature six- and seven-year-olds knew nothing about. I was grateful the fourth and fifth graders mostly sat in the back of the bus and weren't available to spoil our enthusiasm with their knowing condescension.

"Oh, a butterfly from a chrysalis? That's *so* last year. What are you, a baby?"

By the time my parents got home from work, I was practically exploding to tell them. Little did I or they know, we were just a few years away from their having to pry out of my teenaged self anything that happened in school that day. But on that fresh spring day, 10321 Lanett Avenue in Whittier, California, was electric with news of the chrysalis and its movement. Before dinner, I ran the three blocks to our neighborhood library and checked out the World Book Encyclopedia, volume C. For *chrysalis*.

It was all I could do not to open to that page while I was walking, and as soon as I got home, while dinner was being made, I sprawled out on the carpet and furiously turned the pages: *calla lily, cement, chamber* . . . And there it was: *chrysalis*. I read the definition, and next to it I saw four pictures, side by side: the caterpillar, the chrysalis being spun, the dormant chrysalis, and the cracked chrysalis with the emerging butterfly.

I was speechless. My eyes darted back and forth, left to right, going through the sequence of pictures. *That* was what I was going to see the next day. I could not believe this. Mrs. Lambright had told us what was going to happen, but after that stupid caterpillar cloaked himself in that brown stuff and sat still for weeks—well, a girl can give up hope.

Interestingly, Mrs. Lambright had told us what would happen, but she didn't show us pictures until after the butterfly emerged. Perhaps that's part of why the whole experience remains so vivid to me, almost fifty years after it happened.

That night at dinner, my parents allowed me to bring the World Book Encyclopedia to the table, opened to the chrysalis page. They listened as I chattered about what I had seen so far and what I was expecting to see the next morning at school.

I'm pretty sure I slept with the World Book Encyclopedia that night.

My mom wouldn't let me take the encyclopedia to school the next day. (In the eight short years of my life, my overdue fines were already underwriting about 35 percent of the library's operations budget.) But when we got to our room in the morning, we didn't need a book to show us what would happen. Thirty-three third graders (David Coleman was sick that day) walked in to see the marvel of a beautiful and unsteady orange-and-black butterfly testing his new wings in the jar.

For the next few days, the butterfly was the recipient of our near-constant attention. Math slipped by the wayside as we watched and studied and learned about this amazing process we had seen. We put "butterfly food" into the jar (relying solely on Mrs. Lambright's expertise in that area) and kept him until David Coleman returned. It was *unthinkable* that he not be able to see the butterfly.

Then the day came when we took the jar out onto the playground. That afternoon someone got the enviable job of unscrewing the lid, and after a few hesitant seconds, the beautiful creature emerged—this time from the jar into the world he had been created to live in. It was one of the first times I remember having two opposite feelings in my heart: I was happy and sad at the same time. Since then, I have experienced such contradictory emotions many times. But when you are only eight, that's a lot to deal with.

I eventually returned the World Book Encyclopedia to the library (I don't exactly remember, but my guess is that it was late). Soon fractions, field trips, and short-story writing occupied the place our butterfly had previously filled, and our attention was drawn to other wonders.

But there was something magical about that experience that isn't easily replicated, even by other amazing things. That long period of waiting, when it seemed like nothing was happening, was exactly what was needed to change something from ordinary into something quite extraordinary. Years later, when my daughter Mallory was eight years old, she brought home a book on butterflies from school, and I had a chance to vicariously relive my own experience with her.

The whole butterfly thing has been so overdone when it comes to transformation that I hesitated to write about it. But more than the actual transformation, what has stayed with me all these years is the dormancy. The stillness. The perception that nothing was happening . . . which actually turned out to be quite false. But that's sure what it looked like from the outside.

In the biology classes I took in college, we studied what actually occurs inside the chrysalis. It involves mucus and decomposition and other processes that are actually pretty off-putting. But what I still find fascinating is the imperceptible nature of all of that. On the outside, the chrysalis was as still as a dead leaf.

I feel for the caterpillar because I can relate. I might be bored, attending to other things that seem more important than spiritual matters. I might be hurt or disappointed, causing me to distance myself from God. I might be angry—really, really mad—at God, and I simply do not want to talk to him. I might be going through a dry spell; we all have them. For whatever reason, I am far away, disconnected; I am empty and hollow. Sometimes this lasts days or weeks; other times, months and years. In the midst of those times, it seems like these seasons will never end.

And it's never until I emerge, slowly and with great trembling, that I have any hope of looking back and seeing what was happening, imperceptibly, during the dormancy. God's Spirit sometimes makes his presence known in strong and unmistakable ways. But other times he is quiet, almost shy, about the work he is doing in me. Sometimes I am actively involved with him in this soul work. But not during dormancy. Those times, it's all him. There is no cooperation from me, not even a recognition that this gentle work is being done.

I am friends with a woman who, a few years ago, lost her husband. They had been married for just over eighteen years and had three terrific kids. They had a good marriage—not without its bumps, but I haven't seen a good one yet that doesn't have its share. They enjoyed each other; they partnered in life and in parenting. And then, out of the blue, he started feeling sick. Initially his symptoms were vague enough to be dismissed, but eventually they sent him, reluctantly, to the doctor. He kept saying it was no big deal.

But the doctor wasn't so sure, and the tests began. Pretty

quickly the possibilities that presented themselves were grim. It turned out it was an extremely aggressive cancer that had started in his kidneys and had already spread throughout his body. As a couple, they processed this tsunami of information and got second and third opinions. The second and third opinions concurred. It was shocking, devastating, and confusing all at the same time. And time was something they didn't have much of.

They made the decision to start a treatment protocol— one that offered a smidge of hope. But just a few weeks into that, it became clear it wasn't working. And rather than spend his final weeks tethered to an IV that wouldn't help, he came home to die.

If it is possible to help someone "die well," his family did. His family and friends surrounded him, celebrated him, and served him; they sat with him, listened to him, and prayed for him. It was only nine days from the time he stopped treatment and went back to his own bed that he took his last breath. I was at the bedside when it happened, marveled by the strength of those surrounding him and sobered by the moment when he exhaled and no inhalation followed.

The moments and days that came next went much like you'd expect. Disbelief and tears, a million details to attend to in order to honor and bury him, and then . . . silence.

Eventually, everyone has to go home. My friend was supported in significant ways by her family and friends. For weeks and even months, meals came, and people took her out for coffee or went on hikes with her. They babysat and started a college fund for her kids. They were there for her. But eventually, everyone goes home. And the biggest part of grief is yours alone to deal with.

I remember a conversation I had with her over dinner about two years later. She never used the word *dormancy*, but that's exactly what she described. Initially she had been buoyed by people's prayers and presence. Those two things, plus the shock, carried her through the first months of being a widow and a single mom. She couldn't open her Bible, and her restless, wounded soul was unable to sit still. But graciously, her mind wandered to verses she had spent years reading, and they soothed her like a mother rocking an inconsolable child.

And then, without warning, her world went dark. You wouldn't have noticed it from the outside. On the surface, things looked good. She was back to carpooling and packing lunches. She returned to her job and took up tennis. She started combing her hair and wearing makeup, and she even managed to eat enough to put a few pounds back on, replacing her gaunt face with a softer one.

But inside . . . inside, everything was silent. Her soul froze, and she heard and felt nothing. She described it as a kind of "suspended animation." Her body was going through the motions, but there were only echoes where her soul had been.

She had friends she talked to; she had a great Christian counselor who helped her process. But as she said, she found it difficult to process "nothingness."

And then one day, without warning, she had a moment of joy. It was just a moment, less than three seconds, but it was joy nonetheless. It caught her quite off guard. It had been so long since she'd experienced anything like it that it took her almost the rest of the day to sort through what had happened. By that evening, she could name it: *joy*. It wasn't magic; it wasn't complete healing in that moment. It was just a start. Almost imperceptible. It took months and months after that before she came to what she called her "new normal." Where the scars are mostly healed but will never go away.

It was just a crack in the chrysalis—no, not even a crack. Just the trembling movement before the crack. The trembling that signals a new day . . . hope on the distant horizon . . . the lid off the jar.

CHAPTER 9

In Between

*Never doubt in the dark what God
has shown you in the light.*

DR. V. RAYMOND EDMAN

I HAVE A PICTURE OF ME FROM JUNIOR HIGH. How it avoided getting ripped to shreds, I cannot answer. It could be a poster for those years that "only a parent could love."

There I am with an awkward smile, flashing my brand-new braces. I'm wearing cat-eye glasses. In one hand I'm holding a dead pheasant, and in the other? A Sugar Daddy sucker, half-eaten.

In that photograph, I see someone who is emerging from young girl, with teenager coming on the distant horizon. And it's painful. Not mostly from the outside, although I'll give you that. Oh, the inside—ouch. Torn.

Now just so you know, I was mostly not an angst-ridden

teenager, and I rarely felt like I was on a roller coaster of emotions during that time. And yet, even with my internal wiring being mostly stable, there was still a storm a-raging in there! I'd occasionally notice a boy who made my heart flutter, but well, just look at that picture again. That wasn't going to happen. I wouldn't have been capable of deciding between an invitation from him to "hang out" and a strong preference to ride my bike and meet my friends at the store to buy more Sugar Daddys.

It was a stage in my life—one I have *no* desire to return to. That in-between land, coming out of one place and moving toward another, stepping into limbo, unsure of both what's next and how to get there.

It's not just adolescence, either; all middle places are difficult. We're not quite there yet, and we're not sure if "there" will ever show up. Light is rarely at full strength in these middle places. It is dim, at best. You have to squint to see it— really work at it.

A middle place is quite a distance, both from the starting point and from the finish. And although adolescence may have been a lifetime ago, that's not the only middle place we have to live through. I've had many since, and I know there will be more to come.

We are not the only ones who have had to navigate the in-between places. No one knew this better than Moses and the nation of Israel, not long after they left Egypt. For four hundred years, God's people had languished in a foreign land. They were forced to live small, huddled lives in slavery, crying out to God about their oppression. Crying out and groaning.

God told Moses he had heard his people. He told Moses that he was concerned about their suffering and would use Moses to help bring them out of Egypt and into the land he had in mind for them. And then he described the land. It was good and spacious, so verdant and fertile that the land nearly oozed with milk and honey. They would hardly be able to imagine its goodness, and it would be their home. He would take them there.

With the promise of good things to come and relief from their current struggles, Israel turned toward the Red Sea. And on the heels of a series of plagues designed to loosen Pharaoh's grip on God's people, the nation lined up on the shore of the body of water that separated now and then.

In a spectacular show of power, God opened up a way through the water, and when the Israelites trudged up the opposite bank of the sea, they collapsed from exhaustion and exhilaration. What God had said would happen, happened. The Egyptians were behind them, many of them drowned. The sea, too, was behind them. And in front of them? The Promised Land. It was almost too good to be true. For the next several days, the whole nation erupted in song, dance, and festival, repeating words of vindication and God's power. Scripture says that after they crossed the Red Sea, they put their trust in the Lord (Exodus 14:31).

Then the party ended. They packed up, ready to move on. Three days later—*three days*—the complaining started.

I'd like to think that most of my in-between seasons last longer than three days . . .

First they complained about not having water, and God led them to Elim, where there were twelve springs and seventy palm trees. Then it was not having meat. And then their memories became deeply affected, and they started remembering Egypt fondly. Quite fondly. In fact, the way they remembered it, they weren't slaves but rather "sat around pots of meat and ate all the food [they] wanted" (Exodus 16:3). That doesn't sound like slavery or oppression at all. Sounds like a weekend at a great hotel with someone else footing the bill. Yeah, why had they left Egypt anyway? They loved it there!

That's what happens when you're in the middle place. It's not pretty. Your mind starts playing tricks on you. You don't remember so well, but the problem is that you don't remember that you don't remember, and you start getting scared and mad and prickly. You look back over your shoulder, and that time of light—that time when the promises of God seemed so clear and your heart seemed so sure—well, it seems like a lifetime ago. And you get scared and quiet and nervous.

Me too.

But God stilled the Israelites' hearts. Samuel Johnson said, "People need to be reminded more often than they need to be instructed." And God reminded them. He pointed to the substance on the ground each morning—manna that tasted like "wafers made with honey" (Exodus 16:31). He showed them the quail that came each night, providing delectable meat.

For the next forty years, God kept reminding the Israelites. Over and over again. So they wouldn't forget. So the light they received would continue to illuminate them. Because this whole story started with light. Moses, an unlikely hero if there ever was one, was tending sheep in the desert—hardly impressive preparatory work for the future leader of a nation. And it was at that time that the light came to Moses. Sometimes you have to work to find the light, but sometimes the light comes to you.

When Moses saw it, he drew closer to find out if what he thought he was seeing was really what he was seeing. A bush that burned but did not burn up. He'd never seen anything like it before; it was certainly worth a second look.

There was God, with a message and a plan—both of which included a reluctant Moses. And no matter what clarity that light brought, it would need to be renewed. The torch, blazing bright from the bush, would need to be dipped, again and again, back into the light in order for it to be passed on.

Reminders are deeply necessary in those in-between times. The light is fading; it is dim. Then it is gone, just dark. Those reminders come in many forms. Fresh words of encouragement, a sight that stirs the soul, a whisper that all will be well.

And after four hundred years in Egypt and forty years in the desert, they finally arrived. The Promised Land was under their feet: terra firma. But still, the reminders came. In fact, with just a few steps across the border under their belts, they received the first of many reminders: "Watch yourselves closely so that you do not forget the things your eyes have seen or let them fade from your heart as long as you live" (Deuteronomy 4:9). "Return to the LORD," comes another reminder later in the chapter (verse 30). Return, indeed, for the light still burns.

As difficult as life can be, there is still so much goodness, grace, beauty, and joy. The contrast is confusing and almost alarming. But it is also instructive. We are not alone. Generations of people who have followed God have lived in this unfamiliar land, having to learn to live in between. Not just in Exodus and Deuteronomy, but all throughout Scripture. We add our names to theirs.

In Isaiah 42, God speaks words that not only helped Israel thousands of years ago but come to our aid as well. In verses 1-9, the prophet seems to be referencing both the future Messiah and the current nation of Israel. In either case, the arc of this passage is helpful.

For those living in the in-between, the Lord offers this message:

This is what God the LORD says—
the Creator of the heavens, who stretches them out,
    who spreads out the earth with all that springs
        from it,
    who gives breath to its people,
    and life to those who walk on it:

"I, the LORD, have called you in righteousness;
    I will take hold of your hand.
I will keep you and will make you
    to be a covenant for the people . . .
to open eyes that are blind,
    to free captives from prison
    and to release from the dungeon those who sit
        in darkness."

ISAIAH 42:5-7

A few chapters later, Isaiah continues, "Let the one who walks in the dark, who has no light, trust in the name of the LORD and rely on their God" (Isaiah 50:10).

When you are living in between, it's good to be reminded of who it is you trust. God reminds us to consider the heavens and the earth and all the beauty they hold. Their source is the Creator God. As we look at his work, it becomes easier to trust him.

Not long ago, John and I hired a local contractor to do some work on our house. We had heard his name from a few folks in the area, but what sold us was when we got a chance to see his work. We were at a home for an event and were admiring the new construction in one of the rooms. It was really exquisite. Great quality, attention to detail, and work that fit well in that room—not an easy accomplishment. Once we saw his work, we knew we wanted to hire him. His work cemented our trust in him.

When our memory of God's presence is dim, a good, deep

look at his work may restore our trust. Looking around at the magnificent world he has made, even in spite of present circumstances that are difficult, can stir us to remember who we are dealing with. That might give us just a moment of peace or a minute of reassurance, but it is enough.

Isaiah tells us that the same God who created the world we live in and breathe in will hold out his hand to lead us. To take us forward when we cannot see clearly, to bring light that enables those without sight to see. When we have no light, it's good to be reminded that it doesn't necessarily mean there is no light; it's simply that we do not currently see it.

In Luke 1 there are thirty-eight words that beautifully remind us that we are not the only ones who have struggled to live in the in-between, words that show us the light of God in those times.

> The tender mercy of our God,
>   by which the rising sun will come to us from heaven
> to shine on those living in darkness
>   and in the shadow of death,
> [will] guide our feet into the path of peace.
>
> LUKE 1:78-79

These words of praise were spoken by Zechariah, the father of John the Baptist, when his son was born. And why wouldn't he be full of praise? He was an old man and his wife was an old woman when they were told they would have a baby. Zechariah didn't believe it, and he spent the rest of Elizabeth's pregnancy in a silence imposed by the angel who had brought the good news and wasn't particularly fond of Zechariah's response of doubt. When the boy was born, Zechariah unleashed a torrent of praise and excitement about God's faithfulness and his son's role in that. At the end he turned his attention to describing God, saying that we would have forgiveness because of God's tender mercy.

Zechariah knew what it was like to live in between, in long stretches of darkness. Not just during Elizabeth's pregnancy, but for years before that. He'd spent a lifetime in that space between longing and losing hope. Longing to see the Messiah; giving up hope. Longing to have a child; giving up hope. His eyes were dark; he saw no light. Then, when he wasn't expecting it, a glimmer. A glimpse. A piece of light. That glimmer grew into a blinding sun, which would rise from heaven to shine on everyone.

It's interesting to note that Zechariah came from a people who, over the centuries, knew what it was like to live in between. And his people would tell the stories, from generation to generation, to remind themselves that the in-between was just a part of the story, not the whole. That it was really easy to get discouraged, give up, and go down wrong roads when you are in between. But that the light was coming—it really was coming.

Zechariah's father and the generations before him were priests. Priests who constantly told God's people the story of God from the perspective of the rearview mirror. Looking back, they could see God's faithfulness, even during periods of despair, which fostered hope for those in-between times. One of the stories Zechariah's people would have told many times was of the four hundred years of silence.

Referred to now as the intertestamental period, the four hundred years starting with the end of the book of Malachi and ending with the birth of Jesus were silent. There were no words from God, no prophets to point the way. As we look back on that time through the lens of history, it can appear as a simple blip on the radar screen of time. But imagine living in it—imagine living through it. So long without a sound.

But put that feeling together with this description of when Jesus came: "When the set time had fully come, God sent his Son" (Galatians 4:4). The word Paul uses here is *pleroma.* This powerful Greek word means "in the fullness of time." In other words, Jesus came when the circumstances were just right, when a convergence had occurred to make the timing perfect, when the environment and the conditions were exactly aligned.

Well now, that certainly gives another perspective on what those four hundred years of silence might have been about. God, during a period that could be described as a lull, was apparently doing some pretty important work to get circumstances right for the coming of his Son.

To be honest, I rarely look at lulls this way. Mostly, they frustrate me. My guess is that Zechariah and his people must have felt that same way. But what we cannot see while we are in it often becomes crystal clear in the rearview mirror. When the perspective goes beyond my small moment in time and

I consider God's work in the history of humanity, I begin to see other things going on.

The Old Testament closes around 445 BC, when the walls of Jerusalem were completed under the leadership of Nehemiah. Over the ensuing centuries, before that baby was laid in a manger in Bethlehem, the world's stage was being rearranged. Israel fell to the Persian Empire not long after the mortar had dried on the Jerusalem walls. About one hundred years later, Alexander the Great conquered the Persians, and Israel was ruled by the Greeks. During this time, philosophical schools of thought, largely under the influence of Socrates, Plato, and Aristotle, were developed. The whole known world became unified under this cultural shift. The unification movement was resisted by a group of Hasidic Jews who were desperate to retain their traditions of monotheistic worship.

Over the next hundred years or so, the Greek influence waned and Roman rule increased. The Maccabean revolt came at a point when the degradation to the Jewish way of life had reached new lows. At one point Antiochus sacrificed a pig in the Temple at Jerusalem—a grievous offense—as a way to show that he was in charge and what he thought of the Jewish way of life.

To go from the glory of Solomon's Temple, when Israel had a place in the world as a shining star, to this period of national dishonor, when other nations were walking all over Israel, was unthinkable. Over the following two centuries, as Rome's power rose and a succession of rulers from Pompey to

Caesar Augustus to Herod the Great held the Jewish people under their thumbs, Israel was groaning.

Israel, which had always been looking on the horizon for the Messiah, the one God had promised, was searching like never before. Eyes darted back and forth: Where was he? They needed him desperately. They needed a king to overthrow all the bad kings they had languished under.

I surely would have given up. Too long, too quiet. Too many years, too many rulers. But Galatians tells us that God was up to something. That the "fullness of time" was in process to set the stage for Jesus. I'd have missed it—not much doubt in my mind. And I sure as heck wouldn't have been looking for the Messiah in a manger.

As for the work on our house, as much as we trusted our contractor, there were days and weeks when the work seemed as though it would never be finished; it would not emerge looking like what we'd envisioned. But the process grew in us an understanding of waiting, knowing that time was a critical element in fulfilling what we hoped for. It was a slow unfolding rather than a magic-wand moment, an evolving more than an instant in time.

And so it is with life: the understanding that what is happening in the shadows is what is needed to get us to where we long to be.

CHAPTER 10

Before the Dawn

We disappear because we are
uncomfortable with being in process.
MACRINA WIEDERKEHR

LIVING IN BETWEEN IS HARD WORK. It's much simpler to make a choice, color it black or white, draw a line. But even though this living in between is more difficult, it's better. Definitely better.

What lies in the in-between is nuance, richness, and meaning. It's only in the in-between that we can live in color, with heartaches and joys combining hues.

My friends Paul and Ellen lost their twenty-one-year-old son to a drug overdose. Six days after his son's funeral, Paul called me. I asked him how he was doing, and he said that the day before had been his first day back at the office.

"I was pretty much good for nothing those few hours I was there," he said.

"Completely understandable," I told him.

He said, "It's getting harder. The shock and adrenaline are wearing off, and people need to get back to their lives. The reality is setting in that we are living life without Matty."

He went on to tell me about four kids who, since Matt's funeral, had come forward to family or friends to admit that they, too, were struggling with addiction. The rehab center where Matt spent the final nineteen days of his life was overwhelmed by the financial contributions that had poured in, and the staff came to Paul and Ellen to ask how they wanted those donations spent.

"Scholarships," they said. "Assistance for kids who need this help but can't afford it. We're clinging to the hope that we might be able to save *one* kid."

That's living in between. The sorrow I heard in Paul's voice about how it was getting harder, followed by the lilt a few seconds later as he described the impact of his son's death—the ripples and repercussions, the redemption at some level.

My guess is that Paul and Ellen will be living in between till the day they die. Their hearts and minds being pulled in such opposing directions, often in the same moment. Rending. Wrenching.

Living in between forces us to recognize that grief is largely a nonlinear process. There isn't a neat, clean, stair-stepped process that delivers us whole at the end. It meanders, twists, turns, and stalls. Denial, bargaining, and anger turn us around like the spin-dry cycle. Depression invades all the stages. And acceptance? It shows up at some levels, maybe; but in the deepest parts of grief, no.

Time gets all mixed up, and here and there, then and now are barely decipherable. The smallest thing can trigger a memory, and there we are, squarely in the past. The smallest thing can thrust us back to the present with a whiplash-like sensation, and the future becomes almost unbearable to imagine.

Recently, when some friends of ours went through the sudden loss of their child (as Paul puts it, "a club no one wants to be in"), I wrote to Paul. "Tell me," I said, "what to tell them." I think it is those who have gone through it and are going through it who become our teachers in how to help others.

Here's what Paul said in response:

Words can never express the loss this family has suffered—remember that. Sometimes just being with them is more healing than words.

Comfort will come from unexpected places and people; those you expect the most from may be the least involved in your grief.

Forgive those who disappoint you; embrace deeply those who hold you and give you hope, even in the smallest ways.

You will have many people share their story of addiction and/or depression. Listen to them; they have already walked this road.

People will walk alongside you on this journey, but at the end of the day, no one can walk it for you.

Take time with your grief. The second year is tougher than the first.

*People will allow you three to six months to grieve,
and then they go back to their lives.*

*Talk about your loss; frequently use the name of the
one you lost. Do not be afraid to cry a lot and in public.*

*Let people know it's okay to laugh around you and
tell stories; you will be blessed, and they will be more
comfortable.*

*Say yes to every invitation you get so people will keep
you involved in life.*

*Look at pictures and videos only when you want to.
Don't overdo it.*

*Psalm 116:15 has been like a balm to me: "Precious
in the sight of the LORD is the death of His saints" (NKJV).*

*Chris Tomlin's song lyrics, especially "I Will Rise," have
blessed me beyond anything I could ever have expected.*

*The "unexpected visitor" of grief will appear when
you least expect it. It is okay; God is bigger and greater.*

These are holy words, formed from a broken heart that is
clinging to God. I took to heart Paul's first sentence and sent
the rest on to my friend, who was deeply blessed by them.

Paul and Ellen are halfway through their second year of
grieving the death of their son Matty. Their second Christmas
without him is rapidly approaching. During this time Paul
has gotten to know other parents who have been through this
unthinkable journey of losing a child. Seeing some of them
years down the road from the loss, he can glimpse a kind of
hope and healing that he longs for.

The temptation is, knowing that he has experienced some semblance of healing, wanting to leapfrog to that less painful point in the future. But, as he knows, *through* is the only way.

The arc of human history bears out the fact that there are no shortcuts to redemption. God's people, originally planted in the Garden of Eden, quickly found themselves on the other side of paradise. Back and forth between the Promised Land and the desert, we have wandered. God has guided, but he is not quick. There is a slowness to God that belies, I think, his awareness of eternity and our impatience.

Thousands of years after the Fall, God came as an infant to a manger in an obscure village. He spent three and a half years out of a thirty-three-year life in active ministry showing us what the Kingdom of God was really about. Then there were three days between the Cross, the grave, and the empty tomb. Three days that reflect life—pain, sorrow, death, and silence. Waiting. Interminable waiting.

And for those who had loved Jesus most, maybe those days were not even about waiting; maybe they were about giving up hope. Stunned, after spending more than three years with him with a seemingly clear picture of this all ending in triumph, they were now dealing with separation, blood, and a limp body laid to rest, and it was over. Three days may not seem long, but when it's Friday and you don't know how long it's going to be until Sunday, you just know it's over.

There is, between the Cross and the empty tomb, an agonizing silence. Heartbeat-echoing, deafening silence. There is no light. There is not even a waiting for the light. The idea that there would be light again does not register in any neuron of our beings. Minutes tick by, and the truth that it is over sinks in. There is no light. The turn of events is so sudden and unpredicted, so astonishing and excruciating, that darkness swallows the soul. Swallows it whole.

Then the light comes where we least expect it: at the tomb. It's blinding at first, and our eyes have to adjust, much like they do when it's dark. But this is a different kind of adjustment. Where there was death, there is life. Despair gives way, haltingly, to hope. Then to amazement. Then to wonder and awe. Almost too good to be true. This truth has far-reaching, eternal implications for all of us. Death, even death, *does not win*. It is not sufficient to separate us from God.

But in the meantime, we have to live in between. We have to endure those days of relative silence, caught between the kind of life we were created for and the broken form of it we live in. In those dark days between Good Friday and Easter morning, when we wonder if there is any chance for our faith to be resurrected, we have no choice but to sit in the darkness and wait.

The book of Job has been debated, exegeted, and interpreted in many ways. Without getting into the nuances surrounding those critical issues, at the very least Job is a stopping place for those in darkness. Some of the phrases and sentences uttered by Job give voice to our own unthinkable thoughts and inexpressible feelings. These, too, are the word of the Lord, straight from Scripture.

- If only my anguish could be weighed and all my misery be placed on the scales! It would surely outweigh the sand of the seas.
- My brothers are as undependable as intermittent streams.
- Nights of misery have been assigned to me. When I lie down I think, "How long before I get up?" The night drags on, and I toss and turn until dawn.
- My days . . . come to an end without hope.
- My eyes will never see happiness again.
- I prefer strangling and death, rather than this body of mine. . . . My days have no meaning.
- I will give free reign to my complaint and speak out in the bitterness of my soul.
- My face is red with weeping, dark shadows ring my eyes.
- The churning inside me never stops.[1]

My guess is that if we put a line beside each of these phrases (and there are so many more), you could check off at least one of them, having experienced (or currently experiencing) the depths they point to. Perhaps part of what brought Job to the feet of a good and powerful God was his courage to put accurate words to what was going on inside him. That was his invitation for God to touch the innermost part of Job's soul. Nothing was hidden; no pain was held back.

I remember what Dallas Willard said: that the only place God can meet us is in reality. And that if we faithlessly refuse to meet him there, we will simply have no place to receive his Kingdom into our lives.[2] Those phrases from Job? That's what reality looks like sometimes. But we have been misled to think that not only should we not talk that way, but we also shouldn't feel that way.

Sometimes a devoted Christ follower is presented as one who jumps immediately from tragedy into a melodic "God is good!" Powerful words indeed, but in most cases they must be spoken from the other side of pain. When the darkness forces us to the deepest recesses of our souls, it is there that we are able to decide if God is good. No one can answer this for us. They can only tell us about their experiences, and that can be deeply helpful. Or not. As the beautiful line from the musical *The Fantasticks* says, "Without a hurt, the heart is hollow."

And a hollow heart can only give a hollow answer. The words may be right, but the echo gives them away.

This answer about who God is does not come easily or quickly or in one fell swoop. We have to live in reality when reality is the last place we want to live. Initially at least, it's more appealing to live in chirpy praise, even if that is a superficial place. But after a while, the superficial becomes stifling and constricting. It leads to a thin version of ourselves, straining at the edges and brittle.

At some point or another, we eventually need to merge into reality and see what we find.

CHAPTER 11

A Single Beam

It has long been an axiom of mine that the little things
are infinitely the most important.

ARTHUR CONAN DOYLE

BETWEEN HIS CREATION, his miracles, and his name, it is understandable—even expected—that when we think of God, we think big. Eternity? No grounds there for thinking small.

But this bigness includes everywhere and everything. Which implies small, too. And when big is in the small, it's pretty noticeable, memorable, and powerful. If we are going to develop the ability to see in the dark, we will need to be able to shift our attention away from big and toward small, and back again.

Sometimes it is in the waiting for the big that the small ignites into embers of hope. A woman recovering from surgery, waiting to heal before chemotherapy and radiation, trying to wage the rest of the war. She wants to know *now*: Will it work? But what she wants and what she will get at this point are not the same. She struggles long and hard in the unknown, and then one warm afternoon, when her strength is returning, she goes outside for a short walk. She feels the sun on her face, smells the fresh air with its scent of life, sees the flower buds getting ready to unfurl.

She stops, just for a moment, and bends over, looking deeply at that flower bud and breathing in its fragrance. It is just a moment. A small thing, really.

It isn't what she wanted; what she wanted was a clean bill of health. A certificate of chemo completion saying she'd passed with flying colors. She wanted something big. But that's not what she got. She got something small. And in that moment, even though it isn't what she wanted, she knows it is enough. For now. That small thing has calmed her anxious heart, just for a moment. That small thing has reminded her of the beauty of the world and the care God gives to that world. Herself included.

It was the sixth century BC, and the people of Judah thought they were invincible, having recently witnessed the downfall of the Assyrians. Just when they thought they were at the finish, in swooped Nebuchadnezzar from Babylon, and the dream was upended. The people were taken into captivity in Babylon, driven from their beloved homeland as the Temple and their homes were destroyed.

This surely had to seem like a pattern to the Jews. This rhythm of up and down, close and far, winning and losing began to have a familiar ring.

In the Garden, then banished. A people with a promise and a place, to a people enslaved in Egypt. For four hundred years. Back toward the Promised Land, through a round-about way in the desert. For forty years. Crossing over into the land, only to discover it was full of enemies and obstacles, abundance and grace. Over the course of the nation's history, they engaged in battles, had good kings and bad kings, built a Temple, and finally experienced peace.

Sound familiar?

These rhythms over the years, the decades, and the centuries—they're the same rhythms we are acquainted with in the spans of our lifetimes. This is life . . .

The memories that keep us alive also fade over time, and we live between them. This is life . . .

What was even more painful at this time in Jewish history was that this invasion had also resulted in the destruction of the Temple. It may be difficult for us to fully understand what that would have meant to God's people. The Temple was more than just the religious center of the nation; it also served as the hub for commerce, education, and social life in Judah. Their entire society was built around their place of worship. The Temple represented the permanence they so longed for.

And now, not only were they being scattered from their homeland, but their Temple had also been demolished. Their despair was utter and complete. Interestingly, during this time God told his people to put down roots and live deeply in this foreign land (see Jeremiah 29). In the middle of their disappointment and confusion, they were instructed to build houses and plant gardens, to have families and pray for the land they found themselves in. They were to be as content and committed as they'd been in Judah.

Really?

I often find myself coming back to this part of Scripture when I'm going through something difficult. I sometimes say to myself, *If this is my Babylonian exile, how can I go through this with God?*

I also say, *Really?* and a few other things better left out of print. I say all this to God while I am wondering and waiting and wading through the difficulties.

The years passed, and by 538 BC, King Cyrus of Persia had overthrown the Babylonians and started allowing the Jewish people to return to their homeland. The weariness and elation must have been quite a combination. Cautious hope. Tentative excitement. The older folks telling the younger generation what to expect when they traveled back to their Promised Land. Over the next hundred years, in three different groups, thousands of people followed their internal compass home.

Not surprisingly, when they arrived, not everything was as they remembered. The country had been ravaged, and there was much work to do to restore it to its former glory. But they were ready. They were willing. They were home.

But while they were busy rebuilding their houses and

their land, they realized that their Temple lay in complete disrepair. All that was left was a faint outline of the foundation. None of the rocks from the wall were left on top of one another; there was only the imprint in the ground suggesting what had been. The good news of being allowed to return home carried with it subsequent sorrow.

Now let's pick up the story in Haggai 2. Zerubbabel is governor of the province and tasked with rebuilding the Temple. But it wasn't long after the people came to work under his leadership that everyone got discouraged. This was a *big* job. They were barely making a dent. After nearly seventy years of exile, surely someone had a magic wand?

I imagine the Israelites saying, "Seriously, enough is enough. Let's go back to that *big God* concept. We're talking about the one who created the earth, the one who parted the sea. That guy. We've been through enough; we've paid our dues. Now would be a good time for a new Temple to appear right where the old one was."

But as God has shown us over and over, small is the new big. It's where he starts. His power is found in small things—the contrast is compelling. God is there, in those small things that we often overlook when we're looking for God.

Here is what God said to his discouraged people: "Who of you is left who saw this house in its former glory? How does it look to you now? Does it not seem to you like nothing?" (Haggai 2:3).

So not only did God not show up with his magic wand, but he even poked at them a bit first.

Sometimes God is really encouraging—and sometimes he's not. This one goes in the "not" category. It seems obvious from a human perspective that when people are discouraged, a good dose of chirpy cheerleading is what they need. That's not the case here. The people were worn down by the gap they saw, and God asked them to consider that the gap may have been even larger than they thought.

He appealed to the eldest among them. Those with gray hair, achy bones, and a flicker of hope that they would return to see the Temple untouched. Now they were left with the sorrow of knowing they would die without seeing their beloved Temple one more time.

Not so fast, God said. Even though the despair they felt was so strong they were choking on it, here is what he said to them: "Be strong . . . and work. For I am with you" (Haggai 2:4). What a great trifecta for hope.

There was hope in this gap. Hope because God was there.

More of this story is captured in the next book of the Bible, Zechariah. And in this part of the story, God said something pretty bizarre and, I admit, counterintuitive: "The hands of Zerubbabel have laid the foundation of this house; his hands shall also complete it. . . . For whoever has despised the day of small things shall rejoice, and shall see the plumb line in the hand of Zerubbabel" (Zechariah 4:9-10, ESV).

Okay, let's stop here. Because it would be easy to overlook what God was saying.

Have you ever done any kind of remodeling job? A car, a room, a house? To be sure, there are points of excitement in these projects. When you first get the idea, imagining what the improvement will be. Perhaps drawing out the plans or putting on the first coat of paint.

But the plumb line? Nope. No reason for excitement there. It is a small moment in the overall scheme of rebuilding. It's important, of course. The plumb line does vertically what a level does horizontally. It makes sure things are straight. No question this is important. But it's not worth throwing a party over.

But God told his people to rejoice at the sight of Zerubbabel when he showed up with a plumb line in his hand. This verse helps us understand: "Who dares despise the day of small things?" (Zechariah 4:10).

We want big things. God is a big God. But here, in the small and quiet of a plumb line, he is working again. At a point where we might miss his presence, he reminds his people to rejoice. This small moment is a big sign that God is at work.

Do not scorn this moment as unimportant. Do not show contempt for it being "less than." Do not disdain it or look down on it, for it is a sure sign that the work has started.

Small, God says, is *not* unimportant. It is the very building block of important. It's how important is created. It's when a man chooses to respond civilly to his ex-wife even though she poisons every conversation with anyone who will listen. It's small; it doesn't win the battle against her. But it is moving his soul in the right direction. It's when a student, anxious about a test, studies and prays, forgoing the unethical means others around him are using to prepare for the test. Making that small decision sets his choice-making on a course for integrity. It's just a moment, but it's a good one.

It's the stuff a great life is made of. A woman on her way to work leaves just a few minutes early so as not to rush. This enables her, when she has to stop for an elderly pedestrian, to wait with peace rather than exasperation. That small moment ushers in the Kingdom of God as much as any sermon we will ever hear.

Each small right choice is not negligible; it is *hope*. It is not worthless, meaningless, or unimportant. Rather, it is the starting gate going up. It is the celebration of the race begun, and we are a part of it. It is a small thing, by which all things are possible. The Kingdom of God leaking out into the world.

Just a few years later, God's people commemorated the Temple, rebuilt and glorious. The central place of their community, the center of their worship. And then, not long after that, God's people entered into that four-hundred-year intertestamental period. One word that describes those centuries? *Silence.*

And then once again, coming out of the quiet, there was a small light on the horizon. A baby. Born in an obscure village to undistinguished parents and placed in a manger. Once again, the light widens.

After weeks of burning in the dense forest and steep terrain conditions, all that remains of the fire are isolated pockets of smoldering. As the emergency crews pack up their vehicles and tools, they leave behind a scarred landscape looking more like the surface of the moon than a national park.

The worst is over . . . sort of.

Following the nearly forty days of the fire's relentless march through pristine forest, the recovery begins. Looking at it, you'd never guess that recovery was possible. Everything is charred, ruined, and dead.

You and I couldn't see it now, but listen to the words of the area's conservation director: "Next spring is when the visual feast comes in. The burned mountainside will be carpeted with . . . flowers not seen since the last big wildfire in the state park, in 1977: orange-colored fire poppies and yellow-colored golden eardrops. They grow only after intense fires, and there will be millions of them in the burn area."

I've already marked my spring calendar to drive out to see the scene. But between now and then, the recovery will be *slow*.

Almost imperceptible signs of growth and renewal will begin. A small sprout of green, an unfurling fern. The return of insects, animals, and birds that were driven out of their habitat. Water will fall, and the invisible seeds of life buried under the rubble will be stirred to life. Leaves will emerge, and over time, a tipping point will be hit as a riot of color bursts forth onto the decimated land. Hope will be renewed for the future.

Often what emerges out of destruction is life of a deeper and sweeter quality than before. But it takes pain and darkness to get there.

I recently had a rich conversation with an older man at our church. He was one of those rare Christ followers who had grown old well with God. Time alone doesn't guarantee that, but he had made choices along the way to enter the darkness and struggle to find God. His words were full of empathy and truth; his faith was not saccharine or superficial, but rich and deep. He had few easy answers, only an abiding view of the goodness of God.

He had experienced fires of his own. Early childhood scars that had taken him years to even recognize had resurfaced in adulthood in the form of addictions. A deep betrayal in business that harmed his reputation and his bank account, along with some painful seasons with one of his children, had shredded his heart.

I wish you could have been part of the conversation. I was leaning forward, hanging on every word, as he rehearsed his journey. His faith and accompanying doubts, his fears and hopes, his pain. The joy and the wonder, the beauty and the depth in his soul.

He talked about how much Hosea 6 had sustained him: "Come, let us return to the LORD. He has torn us to pieces but he will heal us; he has injured us but he will bind up our wounds. . . . Let us press on to acknowledge him. As surely as the sun rises, he will appear; he will come to us . . . like the spring rains that water the earth" (verses 1, 3).

And then he said this, in his nearly eighty-year-old voice: "I like who I am now much better."

On the other side of the darkness, in the rearview mirror, he could see what had emerged out of those excruciating times, and he clearly saw the hand of God. His love for people was more radically inclusive; his patience, though never his strong suit, was increased, both with others and with himself. Perhaps also with God.

There was new life springing forth from his life. It was, he said, slow, but evident.

Theologian Frederick Faber writes, "In the spiritual life [God] chooses to try our patience first of all by His slowness. . . . He is slow; we are swift and precipitate. It is because we are but for a time, and He has been from eternity. Thus grace for the most part acts slowly. . . . He works by little and by little . . . with a slowness which tries our faith, because it is so great a mystery."

Perhaps this is where the spiritual life is so at odds with the rest of life: in the pace. Eternity has already begun, yet we race around as though our time is limited. God acts slowly over time, in exquisite mystery. We are restless, anxious, driven, and consumed . . . often by all the wrong things.

Faber goes on to say, "There is something greatly overawing in the extreme slowness of God. Let it overshadow our souls, but let it not disquiet them. . . . We must wait for God, long, meekly, in the wind and wet, in the thunder and the lightning, in the cold and the dark. Wait, and He will come. He never comes to those who do not wait. He does not go their road. When He comes, go with Him, but go slowly, fall a little behind; when He quickens His pace, be sure of it, before you quicken yours. But when He slackens, slacken at once. And do not be slow only, but silent, very silent, for He is God."

This is life.

CHAPTER 12

Glimmers

The immortal Spirit . . . is forever tugging us toward him.

CHRISTIAN WIMAN

TWO SUMMERS AGO MY HUSBAND, John, made another of my dreams come true. I had grown up as the only child of an avid fisherman. In general, my father was as avid about hunting and golf (and beer, but that's for another book), but there was something about him when he was fishing that gave me a picture of my dad in his element.

He moved with a grace and patience that was remarkable to me—a kind of quiet dance. He gave great attention to his rods, reels, and tackle box. There was an almost hypnotic quality about him as he scouted out the right place on a lake or river, which would most likely yield a full creel of fish.

I remember his fingers working deftly with the fishing line, tying knots that secured leaders and hooks, as well as the smell of salmon eggs that lingered on our fingers well after the day was done. These were some of my favorite memories with my dad, partly because I had him all to myself for long periods at a time. He loved fishing, he loved me, and he loved teaching me to fish.

I fished lakes and rivers, streams and oceans with my dad. But the one kind of fishing we never tried was fly-fishing.

Years after my dad died, John took me to Montana for three days of fly-fishing, a gift made even more special because . . . well, let's just say John did *not* grow up fishing. We stayed in a small cabin that was part of a lodge, with beautiful views and a shower that required imagination to get wet in.

Each morning after a hearty breakfast, we would set out with a few other guests from the lodge, along with a guide who was not only a genius but actually had neon-green moss growing between his toes. I'm not making that part up—apparently he wore flip-flops all summer that provided the perfect medium for moss to grow. I promise you, it was bright neon green. Fascinating.

All day long, with the patience of Job, our guide would instruct and coach us in the fine art of fly-fishing. I began to understand why this was the only kind of fishing I had not done with my dad. It was fishing on a whole new level.

The interplay between the physicality of the casting and the breathtaking scenery left me lost in thoughts of my dad and grateful to be alive. It was as though time were suspended as I stood in that river, the past and present merging into one.

And then it happened.

The tug.

Almost imperceptible at first, but quickly becoming unmistakable. A quick, staccato yank that moved me from unawareness to awareness. I had completely forgotten that I was fishing.

Quickly setting the hook and beginning to pull in, I saw the glint of sun on the side of a magnificent rainbow trout. It was an exhilarating fight that ended with me holding the fish in one hand and removing the hook with the other. I set the fish back in the water and gently released it, wondering what it would have been like to share this experience with my dad.

Interestingly, as I replayed the day in my mind, it was the tug that stood out. That small moment in time changed my thinking, moved me to attention. A fish on the end of the line, a child reaching up for your hand, a sick woman pulling on the edge of Jesus' garment. Each tug reminding us to stop and take notice, because something is going on here—something we are about to miss if we don't let this sudden movement get our attention. A moment that will pass by if we let it.

Tugs may be among the most profound moments in life. They may awaken us to what is most real, but they come so quickly that we often miss them. A tug was what stopped Jesus in his tracks, saying, "Who touched the hem of my garment?" (Luke 8:45, my paraphrase).

The crowd had been expecting him. Jesus' reputation had spread by word of mouth so rapidly that, not long into his ministry, the throngs of people were already waiting expectantly. Some character named John the Baptist had talked to people about the need for repentance in a way that got loads of them to pay attention. While they were paying attention, he pointed to Jesus and said, "He's the one. The one we have all been waiting for, the Messiah" (see Matthew 3).

Since then, Jesus had been causing quite a stir with the things he said and did. People were definitely paying attention. He had an eclectic mix of twelve guys with him all the time. The messages that were coming out of his mouth lingered with people. Long after they were out of his presence, what he'd said and the way he'd said it stayed with them, tumbling around in their minds and tugging at their hearts.

He kept saying funky things like "Blessed are the poor"; "Those who hunger . . . will be filled"; "Blessed are those who are persecuted"; "Love your enemies, do good to those who hate you"; "If someone takes your coat, do not withhold your shirt from them."[1]

Huh?

His words and his presence kept the people coming back for more. His words and his presence—people talked about them around the watercooler, and then more people came. Before long there were crowds. So often, crowds.

In the middle of one of these crowds, Jesus heard about a synagogue leader whose daughter was very sick; the passage actually says she was dying. This man pleaded with Jesus to come to his house and help his daughter (see Luke 8:40-42).

I won't spend too long on this aside, but if you have a child of your own or if there's a child you love deeply, can you even imagine? Your child is so sick—you know she's dying—and yet there is enough of a glimmer of hope in this man, Jesus, that you would leave her bedside, losing valuable time with her, not knowing if your mission to find him and get him to come back with you will work.

Scripture goes on to say, "Jesus was on his way . . ." (Luke 8:42). The implication here is that as soon as Jesus heard about the dying girl, he turned toward Jairus and said, "Show me the way."

And then on the way, there was a tug. Jesus stopped. He stopped in the middle of something urgent, something that deserved his full attention. He stopped when there was no time to stop. On his way to heal a dying twelve-year-old girl, he stopped to pay attention to a sick and desperate woman. She was trembling, embarrassed to be found out as the "tugger." Embarrassed for others to find out her condition. Embarrassed by the attention when all she wanted was to be healed.

Jesus did—he healed her. He commended her faith; he told her to go in peace.

Then he left for Jairus's house. (In inimitable fashion, hearing that Jairus's daughter had died in the ensuing time, Jesus continued on to see her and then brought her back to life.)

When our kids were little, if they weren't able to get our attention face-to-face, they would often tug at our pants or hands. *Mom, Dad, I know you are talking to someone else or watching something, but I need you to turn your face to me and pay attention to me.* It was all they had before they got words.

We have recently added a yellow lab puppy to our lives. We now better understand what a vigorous and repetitive tug means. Same thing: pay attention to me. No subtlety involved.

Our attention tends to drift and wander and land on what is not important at times. There's no built-in alarm for that, no app to detect it and relay that message to us. Tugs are one of the best ways to help us consider that our attention may not be where it needs to be.

Physical tugs may be more obvious, but tugs in the mind and heart are more profound.

In the mind, these tugs are thoughts and ideas that won't go away. Phrases or concepts that are Velcroed to our brains, refusing to release. They are like rocks in a polishing machine, tumbling over themselves until our thinking smooths them out.

Tugs in the heart hurt a little bit. They are the longings and aches we experience, lasting just a moment before we bury them in something else that doesn't hurt.

It's our choice, really. To stop and pay attention. Or to ignore, dismiss, or deny their message.

Sometimes when I'm busy and my attention is divided and stretched and I feel caught up in a swirl of activities, there will be a tug. When I'm busy, it takes me a long time to pay attention to a tug. Sometimes the tug persists until I do. Sometimes it fades away, and I miss it.

But in those times when I eventually let the tugs do their work, I discover they are often the voice of God giving me one of these messages: I don't need to be this busy; I don't need to be hurried or frantic when I'm busy; he is with me in the busyness and still loves me. He wants me to pay attention to the things that most need my attention.

This is not rocket science, but it's amazing how hard it is to pay attention to the tug and hear the simple message. Really hear it. Hear it in my ears so it goes into my heart and up to my head and out through my life.

Sometimes when I'm lonely, my self-pity party drowns out the tug. Sometimes when I'm angry with someone, my frustration and gossip drown out the tug. Sometimes when I'm afraid, the fear spiral takes me so far down a dark tunnel that I can barely feel the tug.

But these tugs—they are life. They will save me if I'll let them. They are whispers of grace.

It's the things that happen in us when we are stopped in our tracks, when the tug wins, that shape us.

"Is not life more than food, and the body more than clothes? Look at the birds of the air. . . . Your heavenly Father feeds them. . . . See how the flowers of the field grow. . . . If that is how God clothes the grass of the field . . . will he not much more clothe you?" (Matthew 6:25-26, 28, 30). God puts tugs everywhere. It's almost as if in the very design of the universe, there is this magnetic pull to him.

Jesus knew we would worry. He knew that worry reflects more than not trusting God; it is about not *knowing* God. So he pointed our attention to the birds and the flowers.

It's hard to worry without being preoccupied. And preoccupation almost always takes us down the road of not paying attention to the right and true things. We fret over and plan for scenarios that may never occur. We eat too much, or we lose our appetites. We obsess. Our thoughts are like the ball in a pinball machine, bouncing off the walls in random fashion. We spin and whirl.

Jesus knows what is going on inside us, often while the outside looks rather calm. Maybe that's why one of the first things he addressed when he began speaking to the crowds was this problem of worry. He was talking mostly to rural folk who lived what we would consider pretty simple lives. Apparently living in a simpler time and a simpler place doesn't preclude worry. No one is immune.

So Jesus draws our attention to birds and flowers—things we are likely to come across nearly every day. He says that when we take time to consider the birds, we realize that, without any forethought of their own, without planting and harvesting crops, they are fed and cared for. Something—someone—beyond themselves is providing for them.

Then the flowers. Linger for a moment and look—really look. Their splendor and beauty are evident, yet they did not create those traits themselves. God clothes them.

When we listen to Jesus teach lessons about worry in the presence of birds and flowers, it goes beyond just what we hear. It creates a future tug. Sometime, when you're not even thinking about his teaching, a bird may flit across your field of vision, or out of the corner of your eye you may see a magnificent, delicate flower. And you may find yourself experiencing a pull to consider what that might mean in your life today, given your circumstances.

Of course, it may not be a bird or a flower. It could be just about anything—something we see, hear, or think about. Since we live in a world God created, tugs are everywhere. We're only "safe" if we ignore them, but given what they have to offer, why would we? The trick is to let them help us dig deeper. And pause. Sometimes it's only a moment, sometimes a bit longer. Sometimes we keep coming back to the tugs to let them do their full work.

When I was fly-fishing with John in Montana, in between snagging one of the six fish I caught (Oh, John? He caught five.), I let the physical tug I had felt with the fish allow me to pay attention to the heart tug that the experience and the scenery were bringing to me.

For just a couple of minutes, while I was by myself in the rushing river, standing in my waders, I let everything in. The tug was there, but I was afraid if I opened myself up to it, I might not recover.

On that sun-bathed, blue-sky, glorious day, surrounded by the peaks of the Continental Divide and the spring-green grass carpeting the ground, I allowed the tug to take me away.

And for just a few minutes, I felt marvelously overwhelmed by the sheer beauty of the world, by the goodness it speaks of its Creator. I felt marvelously overwhelmed by the gift of my dad and fishing with him as a little girl and eating trout sandwiches from our bounty. I felt marvelously overwhelmed by the idea that all this might be only a sliver of what it reflects. Eternity. Good. God.

I think I was right: I haven't recovered.

CHAPTER 13

Light,
Darkness, Light

Love is so great, is to be half afraid—
It is like looking at the sun
That blinds the eye with truth.

JOHN HALL WHEELOCK

AT THE STARTING GATE AND THE FINISH LINE, there is light. In Genesis 1, God's first recorded words were "Let there be light." In Revelation 21, as John describes the new Jerusalem, he says the light that illuminates this great city comes from the glory of God. The final chapter of Revelation says that the Lord God will give the inhabitants of this new city light and that there will be no darkness there.

Light is a beautiful and desperate metaphor. Ushering in the grand act of creation, illuminating everything. In strength by day; in soft reflection by night. The very nature of light teaches us about the goodness, strength, and presence of a God so far beyond us that it is difficult to know him.

Combating that distance, light becomes embodied in Jesus so we can see, touch, and hear it. This Light revealed himself in such a compelling way that Peter, who followed Jesus closely, was prompted to say, "Where else could we go but to *you*? You have the words of eternal life; you are the holy one of God" (John 6:68-69, my paraphrase).

Jesus said, "I am the light of the world" (John 8:12). We are most aware of our need for light when it is dark.

Although it is dramatic that the Bible starts and ends with light, it is sobering to realize that there is a lot of darkness in between. In rhythms that wax and wane, the light and darkness dance as uneasy partners. Often the darkness overtakes, and the light seemingly disappears. There is aching and despair, questioning and pleading, deafening silence and pain.

Not long after the light that ushered in Creation appeared, there was darkness. The people God created chose sin, and they were banished from living with him in the Garden. Everything that was once so perfect had gone so terribly wrong, so soon.

Yet even then, even in the darkness that fell, there was a glimmer of light. The promise of Jesus' coming. Just a verse tucked away, overlooked in the midst of the pain and dwindling light (see Genesis 3:15). This glimmer expanded over the centuries, often imperceptibly, but growing nonetheless.

The alternating light and darkness continued to dance across the arc of time and history. Light with the promise of Isaac, born to Abraham in his old age; darkness on the altar that Abraham placed him on. Darkness in Egyptian exile and slavery; light from the burning bush that pushed Moses to lead the people out. Light for God's people in the crowning of David as their king; darkness as sin invaded his life and moved the trajectory of his influence in another direction. Light at the height of the Israelite nation's glory under Solomon; darkness under the oppression of Babylon. Darkness in the four hundred years of quiet; light, just a glimmer, barely perceptible, in the manger in Bethlehem.

Then the light widened. The people saw Jesus—what he did. They heard Jesus—what he said. He declared himself the Light of the World, and in that light they saw who he was: the holy one of God.

The light grew as his ministry, following, and influence grew. Those who followed him held on to the belief, almost unshakable, that Jesus was on the precipice of leading them into the nonstop glory of Israel's future. Then darkness descended into more darkness as the days led to the garden of Gethsemane and Jesus' arrest, conviction, and crucifixion.

Dark beyond dark. Startling in its intensity. *How were we so wrong?* The darkness was so suffocating that it drew denials and caused dispersal and hiding. The darkness was so deep that it seemed permanent. There was no light.

The few who stayed with Jesus watched as the soldiers took his lifeless body from the cross, even as rigor mortis was setting in. The spices were applied and the body was carried to the cave, placed inside, and sealed with a stone whose weight marked the finality of this day.

It was over. Soul-wrenching quiet . . . silence. He was

gone. There was darkness everywhere. Shock settled in as those who had followed Jesus with such hope realized it was over. Done. Fade to black.

Then came Sunday morning. Before they even saw it, the light was back. Before it had hit the rods and cones in their eyes, it had returned. This light, which had once been a glimmer of promise in Genesis, was now in full force in the risen Christ. The power of this light was inextinguishable. Its photons emanate into our reality, into the twenty-first century.

Our lives, too—yours and mine—have this rhythm of light and darkness. The light fades; then it brightens. The good and bad, the easy and difficult exist together, sometimes in the same space and other times with one overtaking the other. But still, the light is there, stronger even in its lesser forms than the darkness. That is the promise of Jesus, the Light of the World: he overcame every kind of darkness, even death, the final form of darkness.

In 1 Timothy 6, Paul reminds the young Timothy to persevere: "Take hold of the eternal life to which you were called" (verse 12). He tells Timothy that God lives in "unapproachable light" (verse 16) and then concludes his letter by telling Timothy what happens when we live in that light: "[We] may take hold of the life that is truly life" (verse 19).

In the darkness, it's easy to miss what is truly life. The darkness begs us to settle for a knockoff. It wants to cheat us. It wants us to wrestle ourselves out of the darkness so quickly that we fail to stay there and wait . . . wait for the light to show us where next to put our feet. It tricks us into easy answers and superficial directions, all the while leaving us hungry for the life that is truly life.

Peter puts it this way: "You are a chosen people . . . that you may declare the praises of him who called you out of darkness into his wonderful light" (1 Peter 2:9).

His wonderful light—light that offers us the life we were created for. Light that comes out of and into our darkness.

CHAPTER 14

Light Finds a Way

*The soul can split the sky in two and
let the face of God shine through.*

EDNA ST. VINCENT MILLAY

A RAY OF LIGHT SHAFTS THROUGH A ROOM, making sparkling bits out of dust. Light bends in the wet sky, making a rainbow. The sun's first rays break over the horizon to usher in the day. Light touches our souls: we pause, we ache, we hope.

The light reflects off the ocean, and as we emerge from the water, that same light warms our skin. The sunset bends the light into coral, pink, and crimson as the light fades, ending the day. Lightning cuts through the sky, thunder tumbling into the hole it leaves.

Light, intensely focused, lasers through malignant growths, bringing wellness. Light makes its way through strands of glass to create the pulse of the Internet, connecting the world.

Physicists tell us that in the future, we may ride the "winds of light."

When light enters our eyes, it registers objects upside down. Ironically, the brain is encased in bone with no way for light to enter. Yet approximately one-fifth of it is devoted to capturing and translating light, and it corrects those images, causing us to see things right side up. We don't actually see light, but we need it in order to see everything else. Light is inscrutable. A wave, yes. A particle, yes. In a linear way, it behaves in one fashion; when bent, absorbed, or refracted, it acts in another way. It is at the same time obvious and mysterious. And the light we can see with our eyes, compared to the full spectrum? It's very small.

When electrons dance, they release photons, which in turn emit light. And like a river, light finds a way. Nearly unstoppable. Powerful. From a sunset to a treatment for cancer to a remarkably linked world.

In the beginning, God said, "Let there be light." And there was light (Genesis 1:3). He created it; then he used its nature to teach us, to show us the way. It is not just a physical asset but also a metaphor. God created it in order for us to use it, and as we use it, to learn about it. And in our learning about it, to learn more about the God who made it. It is a visible symbol of the presence of the unseeable God. He uses light to brighten our days, grow our food, warm our bodies, and resonate in our souls as we search for meaning and follow him in the darkness.

A few years ago my heart was in tatters. When you are a parent, nothing hurts as much as the referred pain stemming from your child's pain. If I could have changed places with my child? Not even a question; absolutely. If I could have fixed it for my child? *Yes.* But I knew none of that was possible. I even knew none of that was truly optimal. If you take people's problems away, they don't grow; they don't become the kind of people they could be. But in that moment, I didn't care about this truth. All I knew was that my child (okay, my twenty-something-year-old, but still) was in pain, and I would have done anything I could to change that.

We spend much of our lives learning that we are not nearly as in control as we thought we were, but that's most difficult to accept when it affects our children. Partly because, when they are fresh and new, just wiped clean of amniotic fluid and bundled in a soft blanket for the first time, control is exactly what a parent brings. It is a gift of protection for these infants who cannot yet protect themselves. Control is a big part of what it means to be a good, responsible parent—at least in the beginning.

You control their eating; you control their environment. You protect them; you make decisions for them. Most of what they experience comes from your direction. And that control, necessary when they are small, sets you up for anxiety over anything untoward that could happen to them. Because although they have only been in your life a short time, you have already discovered that your soul would be shattered if any harm came to them.

As they grow older, that balance shifts, but no one—and I mean *no one*—can tell you exactly when to put in the clutch and change those primal gears and begin to let go. And it's not like you put in the clutch once; you have to do it multiple times. It makes for a pretty bumpy ride.

So I took my tattered heart, in all its pieces, to the home of a woman in our church who leads our prayer team. She is responsible for the oversight of scores of people who feel deeply called to prayer and who make themselves available to folks right after our church services to pray with them.

She is also a friend of mine. She has gone through deep valleys herself, one of which was her son's cancer diagnosis and treatment when he was a teenager. Cancer in any form is devastating, and his was especially troubling in someone so young. He is now in his midtwenties, and after more than a year of difficult treatments, he is cancer free and thriving. But my friend knows what it's like to pray in the dark, when you don't know if there will be a happy ending.

There is something about praying with someone who has gone through such pain. She offered me no easy answers, no quick remedies. Just prayer. She guided me through talking to God, which was no small thing, because this was difficult when my pain was so great.

I was at her house for about an hour. We spent the first few minutes catching up, and then she took me to the sitting area in her bedroom, which had big windows overlooking their beautiful backyard. We stopped to admire a few family photos of her and her husband and their three kids, and then she offered me a seat in an overstuffed chair—the kind that swallows you up and hugs you when you sit in it.

The sun was streaming through the windows, bringing its own kind of comfort as I sat there listening to her. "So I'll ask you to close your eyes, just to free you from as many distractions as possible."

And then she told me she wanted me to picture Jesus and what he might have for me in this difficult situation.

Then she let it be quiet. It was painful but necessary. My heart, in so much pain, wanted my body and my mind to keep moving to distract me. Perhaps distraction is necessary at times. Silence, stillness, and quiet, while extraordinarily helpful in times of crisis, are not the only things that help. And one can't stay in silence, stillness, and quiet all the time. But those moments become pieces of healing to help us merge back into life with all its activity.

Here's all I knew in that moment. I was only going to be there another thirty minutes or so, and of that time, most likely about half of that time would be spent talking through what I experienced during my reflective time. So, right then, sitting in that chair in the quiet she was instructing me toward, I only had about eight to twelve minutes . . . with nowhere to go and nothing I could do to change my situation. Finally my heart and mind agreed to be still.

In that short period of time, here's what my mind's eye saw.

For a while, all was just dark, pretty reflective of how my insides felt. Dark and quiet. And then, Jesus. Probably mostly because my friend had asked me to picture him and to consider what he might have for me. But there he was, and there I was. We were facing each other. I was smaller than he was, and there were a few yards between us.

I don't think I said anything to him—I just reached behind me and pulled my child between him and me. I simply looked at Jesus. I was pretty sure he knew what I was asking. And then, as if tethered by elastic, my child sprung back behind me.

Multiple times I reached back and brought my child between Jesus and me—after all, that was why I was there—but each time my child sprang back behind me. Slowly, without hearing any words, I began to understand that for Jesus, this was not about the child. It was about him and me.

Then I noticed that there was a bit of light present—just enough to illuminate the few yards between him and me. Nothing more.

This was not the answer I wanted; it was nowhere near what I'd come looking for. I wanted more light—for me and for my child. My multiple attempts to put my child between Jesus and me were my way of trying to get him to see that. Then, at last, I stopped. Stopped trying to make this all about my kid, stopped frantically trying to get Jesus to see what I was showing him. Just stopped.

And in that stopping, my heart heard, *This is about you and me. And the only light you need right now is the light you see. The light that shows you the steps toward me. If you let that be enough, your heart will be at ease. Your grip on control will slacken, and you will live in that bit of light, which is the right place for you to live right now. That small piece of light will enable you to be with your child in a nonanxious way and let me do my work. If you move out of that small piece of light, the darkness will be great. You must find a way to live here and to find your way back here when you move away.*

That was all. It was just a few minutes—four or five at most. Then for ten minutes or so, my friend and I talked about what I'd experienced. Then I walked to my car to reenter my life.

The peace that emerged following this experience was deep but temporary. Indeed, I did have to keep working and wrestling to find my way back to that place, because I wandered often. But I knew that what I'd learned was life. I knew I had to fight to keep it. It was peace without resolution or promise of outcome. It was following the light I'd been given. It wasn't nearly as much as I'd wanted, but I was beginning to understand the disproportionate power in that small piece of light.

The very nature of light provides contrast. In juxtaposition, differing levels of light illuminate in extraordinary ways, helping us to see what we've been missing.

In the late 1400s, the art world made a giant leap forward when some of the painters, sculptors, and woodblock printers of the era began to experiment with shading and using light in ways that began to achieve a sense of volume and dimension in their work. *Chiaroscuro*, it's called. Light and dark together, side by side. They found that the contrast affected the whole composition, the interplay of light and shadows creating an emotional response in those who viewed these works.

More than anything, this proximity of light and dark in a work created perspective. Moving from flat to three-dimensional, creating a more accurate depiction.

Hundreds of years later came a chiaroscuro of sorts in medicine, as physicians moved from X-rays to 3-D imaging, which gives a much more accurate view of what is happening in the body. Light and darkness, side by side, providing a contrast for better perspective.

And so it is in our lives: chiaroscuro for the soul. Light illuminates the darkness, in shades and shadows, giving just enough brightness to provide depth and understanding. Seeing the two side by side allows us to appreciate how the light illuminates the darkness, how the darkness makes the light more vivid.

Sitting in the chair in Beth's room that day, moving through that short time of guided prayer . . . this, too, was chiaroscuro. Hundreds of years after the artists employed this technique, here I was, drinking it in. Needing it. The darkness didn't go away, but it was amazing how such a little piece of light made a difference. The darkness was what eventually drove me to God. Pleading at his feet, wrestling, arguing, venting. Ashamed, confused, desperate.

I wanted enough light to erase all that. Enough light to blind everything and take over. But I learned to live in the light that was given. And it was enough.

Five years later, my child was through the pain. Five years when I lived on a sliver of light. The sliver that kept me where I needed to be.

Now, one year after that season of heartbreak ended, I find that the contrast between the darkness and the light has sweetened life for me. It has solidified the ache in me that curses the darkness, that knows at a visceral level that we were not made to live in the darkness. Since we have been created as creatures of light, the darkness tears at everything noble in us. And well it should.

I now know in my soul how powerful light is. How a small amount can bring such relief and hope. I now know that if so little can overcome so much, the power is clearly in the little.

In Exodus 33, Moses finds himself in a frustrating position. Not long before, he had encountered God in the burning bush and had begun to understand his role in leading God's people out of a four-hundred-year captivity in Egypt toward the Promised Land—the place of God's promise. This task seemed daunting enough; it was probably a good thing God didn't lay out for Moses what would happen after he got the Israelites out of Egypt.

I'm guessing that when Moses finally got on board with this whole thing, he was thinking his main challenge would be to muster up the courage to ask Pharaoh to let his vast network of free slave labor leave. And now that he had Aaron to help him with this "ask," things were looking up. Surely it would be smooth sailing up north once they crossed Egypt's border.

But from the very beginning of his assignment, Moses experienced a constant push and pull. There were the plagues, then Pharaoh relented to "yes." This was followed by a change of mind to "no"—and then more plagues. By the end of ten plagues, the Egyptians were practically begging the Israelites to leave. At least until they got as far as the Red Sea, and then Pharaoh had another change of mind, enforced by an army of chariots and soldiers in pursuit.

Once the Israelites made it to the other side of the Red Sea, out of Egypt's reach, there was quite a party. Exhilarated, exhausted, and relieved, they sang their thanks to God. Most likely they fell asleep thinking, *All that's left now is to rest up and then make the few days' journey through the desert into the land of Israel. Home.*

It was four hundred years of slavery later, but better late than never. They were almost home.

But these people, loved by God though they were, were not yet ready for that home. Quickly after recuperating from escaping Egypt, the complaining began.

I have been captivated by the book of Exodus for years. Even as a child, I recognized the people's immaturity in complaining so soon after they'd seen God work in amazing ways. I also recognized that while I might sit in judgment of them,

I'd most likely do the exact same thing. Perhaps "would have done the same thing" would be more accurate.

So they complained about the lack of food and water; they complained about the quality and frequency of the food and water. They encountered enemies, and suddenly this exiled group of slaves had to become an army.

They listened as Moses brought down God's Ten Commandments to give them a moral guide as they became a nation. Together they fashioned and built a portable place of worship so that as they moved through the wilderness that separated them from their home, they would remember the God who was leading them.

Then there was a bit of a turning point, a hinge. It seems that it was dawning on Moses that this was not going to be a quick, simple journey, but rather a long and circuitous one. As in Exodus 4, when Moses pleaded with God to send someone else to have this conversation with Pharaoh and God gave him Aaron, Moses once again came before God. "You have been telling me, 'Lead these people,' but you have not let me know whom you will send with me. . . . If your Presence does not go with us, do not send us up from here" (Exodus 33:12, 15). When God assured Moses that his presence would indeed be with them, Moses still wasn't satisfied. Maybe it was the gap between how difficult he thought all this would be and how difficult it actually turned out to be, but the bottom line was that he wasn't taking one step further until something more dramatic happened. Until he *saw* God.

"Now show me your glory" (Exodus 33:18). Moses was clear on what he wanted to see.

God was clear on what Moses couldn't bear to see.

They were the same thing. *God.*

"You cannot see my face, for no one may see me and live" (Exodus 33:20).

It was as if God were saying, "The amount of light you can take in and the amount of light I Am—they are too disparate. You are not capable of exposure to the full expression of God. Just a sliver is all you can assimilate."

So God hid Moses in a fissure of a rock. Rock that could keep light from penetrating, protecting Moses. Even with that protection, God said, "I will pass by and you will see only the trail of what is left after I have passed by" (Exodus 33:22-23, my paraphrase). That's as much as Moses could handle and not be dissolved. But that's also as much as he needed.

Just a sliver. Just a small amount of the light that is God will get you all the way through the desert. It will get you all the way home.

CHAPTER 15

Benediction

benediction *(Latin): bene (well); dicere (to speak)*

AT THE END OF OUR CHURCH SERVICE, Dave Peterson gives the benediction. When I was growing up, the benediction in our church was fairly perfunctory. It seemed to be a collection of rather bland, vague words meant to close the service and signal our exit. It wasn't until I experienced the benedictions of Dave Peterson that I understood the power in these blessings.

I honestly think people go to Dave's services for the benediction. I think they would pay for them—I know I would. Something about Dave's presence and thoughtful, heartfelt words offer hope and healing. They sum up what we have experienced together and feel like the very best leftovers, wrapped up in anticipation of enjoying another meal. These words allow us to take the experience with us and change us beyond Sunday.

Dave quotes Scripture with such an easy familiarity that you know he has lived in it. The timbre of his voice extends a nonanxious presence, and his words are full of the deep love of God. He has lived in joy and pain, with God. And his benedictions make you want to do the same.

Benediction is a deeply rooted custom in the Christian church, having even deeper roots in Jewish tradition. The ancient Jews understood the importance of final words following a time of being together. These were people who knew well that when they dispersed, there were few guarantees of what life held until the next time they gathered together.

Persecution, famine, lack of clean water, enemies, and disease all meant that the group that had just met would most likely be minus a few the next time. These final words were words of power. Words that connected them to what they'd just experienced and the meaning of that experience . . . until they met again.

These words invoked God in order to wrestle a blessing from him, as Jacob had done. They were memorable final words that would ring in people's hearts and ears as the week wore on, reminding them of their collective experience as God's people. This benediction would also get them ready for the week as they dispersed. The words were magnetic—words that would draw them together again.

And these words of benediction remind us what has the last word. It is light. As dark as the dark gets, over time what emerges is the strength of hope, the fierceness of the good. We each come to church from very different places. When we leave, what is finally poured over our heads is light. The final word that will prevail is *God*.

Last weekend I was part of a gathering of mostly African American church leaders. At one point a young woman, whose voice has graced opera stages, sang from the music genre she referred to as Negro spirituals. The words were rich with suffering, flowing out of hundreds of years of abuse and pain. But the threads that wove through every verse were perseverance and deliverance. The view was toward the horizon and the light that waited there.

Our oldest daughter, Laura, married Zack nearly four years ago. When they leave our house after we've spent time together as a family, one of us will say to them as they walk out the door, "Take good care of each other." It is our benediction over them—words of love and power to guide them until we see them again. It is a prayer of blessing over them— a reminder that while we all take care of ourselves, in a deeper way we also take care of one another.

These words were not deeply thought out or premeditated. One night someone said them, and they stuck. Probably because they were words with just the right touch. They seemed to sum up our hopes for them when they were away from us.

But other times a benediction is wrenching.

Not long ago I watched one of my best friends from high

school give a benediction. It was at the funeral for his twenty-
one-year-old son.

It had been a while since we had talked when Paul called
me on Mother's Day. When his name came up on my phone,
I was expecting some funny intro, but what I got was silence.
I said his name a couple of times, thinking we had a bad connection. And then he told me.

His words were halting but firm, and at the end there was
a catch in his voice. I felt both disbelief and the sensation of
swallowing a brick. We talked for the next thirty minutes,
and soon my disbelief gave way to tears. The brick didn't give
way, though; it stayed. It's still there as I write this. I don't
know when the brick will go away. I know that for Paul and
his wife, Ellen, it never will.

I met Paul my freshman year of high school. And in that
way that is difficult to explain, we just clicked. He was the
brother I never had. We went hunting and fishing together.
We made jokes in class and evaluated who the other was
dating to be sure the person met our standards of approval.
We did class projects together, hung out at each other's
homes, and stayed in touch, if sporadically, through these
forty-plus years.

Paul and Ellen had two boys, Miles and Matthew. Miles
was twenty-five when his younger brother, Matthew, died.
Listening to Matt's friends tell stories at the funeral service, I
got the sense that he was a breezy character who lit up a room
just by walking in. He was that unusual kid who was able
to weave between all the different cliques in high school and

bring disparate groups together. He paid no attention to the differences in people, and he made friends wherever he went.

And a few months before he died, he told his folks he thought he needed to go to rehab.

This was the most startling sentence Paul and Ellen had heard out of the mouth of either of their boys. Thinking he may have been dabbling in marijuana, they listened as he unfolded his months-long descent into the grip of heroin.

That sentence immediately replaced the first as the most startling one they'd ever heard.

After nineteen days in rehab, he was released, having been dubbed an exemplary patient. The next morning he was dead of an accidental overdose.

That evening around nine o'clock, there was a knock on Paul and Ellen's door. Paul says he sensed an inward voice telling him calmly, *That will be the police. They are here to tell you your son is dead.*

It was, and they did.

Over the next seventy-two hours, buoyed by the adrenaline that shock produces to protect the body, Paul and Ellen made phone calls and planned a memorial service.

Toward the end of my phone conversation with Paul, he mentioned his eulogy preparation. I listened, but I could hardly imagine how a father would go about preparing words as a tribute to his child. His boy. His towheaded, high-spirited Matt. I remembered hearing the joy in Paul's voice, the pride, when Matt was born. I know there were the nights he held Matt, snuggled against his neck as he rocked him to sleep.

The mornings of teaching him to ride a bike, the afternoons of baseball practice, the evenings of dinner and homework. The glorious ordinary.

Paul ended our conversation by talking specifically about the benediction. He had opted to do that part of the service as well, saying that as Matt's dad, it was his responsibility to say good-bye to him. I hardly knew how to process what I was hearing.

Paul was determined that the good in Matty's life would get the last word. The darkness was great and in danger of overwhelming him. But Paul believed that the darkness would not win. The darkness was not all that he was experiencing. Even in the midst of what were surely the darkest days of his life, the light was stronger.

At the service, when I listened to Paul's words of benediction, I heard my dear high school friend say good-bye to his son. I didn't know Matt well—mostly through stories Paul told me as we kept in touch over the years. Paul and Ellen had moved from California to Ohio, and the distance kept me from knowing their sons in a personal way.

My pain was the pain of a friend. The heart-heavy sadness of listening to my friend benedict the life of his son. The "brick in the stomach" feeling that my friend, as he grows to be an old man, will be an old man who lost a son.

Those final words, when spoken aloud, marked the end of a life that had already ended. But the formal words of benediction in the service were not Paul's final words to Matt. At the graveside, when the crowds left, Ellen and I were sitting in the car when Paul got out of the driver's seat. Without a word, he slowly made his way to the rose-covered casket. He was far enough away that we could not hear the words he was saying, but we could see his lips moving. His face was contorted with grief, and my stomach-brick grew.

It wasn't long before he slipped back into the car and turned the ignition. Later that day, as Paul drove me to the airport, I asked him what he'd said to Matt.

"I told him I forgave him. And I asked him to forgive me."

A benediction indeed.

There is a power in last words. Something in them distills what is most important. Entire books are written on last words; they seem to deeply reflect the soul of a person. There is deep meaning attached to them, and they can offer hope in the face of great loss.

I lost my grandmother Gladys when my youngest child, Johnny, was two weeks old. She was eighty-eight and had recently been diagnosed with lymphoma. She lived about four months between her diagnosis and her death. The only symptoms she had early on were tiredness and shortness of breath. Really, who's *not* tired at eighty-eight years old?

She found herself unable to keep up with her usual routine, which included driving her 1968 eight-cylinder Mustang to do errands and raking the leaves from the magnolia tree in her front yard. That tree was the bane of her existence, dropping its large leaves on a near-daily basis.

That last month she spent most of her time in a hospital bed that was delivered to her house, and my aunt and my mother rotated caring for her. One of the conversations I had with her when she first took to that bed was about how ready she was to go. Ready to be out of a body that was failing her and that ached at every turn. She had lived a good life and was looking forward to seeing the husband she'd lost so many years ago.

Two weeks before she died, I gave birth to Johnny. During our first few days at home with him and his two sisters, Laura (three and a half) and Mallory (eighteen months), John and I planned a weeklong vacation for the following month. We would stay with my parents, who lived a few miles from my grandmother, and spend time with our extended family and our just-finished family.

A week before that vacation, I made the ninety-minute drive to visit my mom for the day, taking Johnny with me. John had the girls, and it felt great to get out of the house with only one kid. (Why is it that no matter what number of children you have, as soon as one kid is with someone else, it feels so much easier?) I decided to get on the road by mid-afternoon to beat the always-present LA traffic. As I headed to the freeway on-ramp, I vacillated on whether I should swing by my grandmother's house and make a quick visit with the baby since she had not yet seen him.

Mostly I thought no, seeing as how we would be there for our vacation in just a short time, but at the last minute, I turned my car onto Pioneer Boulevard and drove to that familiar house from my childhood. I unbuckled my newborn son from his car seat and surprised my aunt when I walked through the door.

We chatted for a few moments, with her updating me on Grandma and me giving her a play-by-play of my intense four-hour labor. She held Johnny and we talked until we heard Gladys stirring, now awake.

I went in and sat on the folding chair next to her hospital bed. Her face was puffy, and I could tell by the way she held her mouth that she was in pain. I talked to her softly, brushing her hair off of her face and offering her sips of water through a straw.

It was hard for her to talk, so I held Johnny up for her to see him. Her eyes lit up and focused on him. She said only two things.

"I wish I could hold him."

She was so weakened at this point that even turning from one side to the other was too enormous of an effort. She couldn't hold a cup of water. And she couldn't hold Johnny, her newest great-grandchild. But she could, and did, drink him in with her eyes. For probably forty-five seconds, those two with Boatright blood in them locked eyes. His eyes were learning to focus for the first time; hers were rapidly losing that ability. His breath was close to his first inhale; hers was close to her final exhale.

"He's beautiful, honey."

Four days later, Grandma died. Peacefully, my aunt said. Had I waited for our vacation, I would have missed that visit.

It would have been okay if I had, but I'm glad I didn't. And I'm glad she didn't. To this day, I savor those last words she said to me. And although her imminent death felt like a small darkness descending, she left behind a piece of light.

Her words were her final shelter over me. She had been a steady presence in my young life when my home was tumultuous. As I got older, I was able to see even more clearly the strength and depth of her soul, her near unshakability. And I think that just by being near her all those years, I had some of that steadiness permeated into me. Just a bit. Just enough.

From generation to generation, the light is passed on like a torch. My grandmother, who had been such a light to me during my life, had words of light on her lips, even in her death.

A benediction. When all is said and done, these are the final thoughts we are left with. These are God's words to God's people. These are the good words of blessing God would like you to have stuck in your mind and heart, to revel in over the next hours and days. These are the lingering thoughts of God.

Two weeks ago, a good friend of ours died. He was not just a friend; he was good. In so many senses of that word, *goodness* described his center. He was not a perfect person, but when we were with him, we felt calm. Centered. Deeply convinced of God's goodness.

Sometimes when we would leave, he would benedict us.

He would speak over us words of power, words of blessing, words reminding us of the goodness of God. And those words would linger in us. Long after we had left his presence, our souls would be strangely calm, covered by the words he spoke like a canopy over us.

Another friend was with him in the last hours before his death. This person told us our friend's final words: "Thank you." Not spoken to anyone in particular, just "Thank you." This didn't surprise me at all. But it moved me. It was the benediction of his life.

And his words have stayed with me. They are so reflective of his nature—there is an authenticity and a congruency in this final statement. In the past couple of weeks, I have thought about what kind of life you would have to live so that in the midst of an awful death, a wretched disease, "Thank you" is what comes out of your lips.

A benediction becomes a meditation of sorts. Not the kind of meditation where you sit in stillness and quiet, but a moving meditation. Words that rattle around in your heart and mind, refusing to let go because there is so much meaning in them, so much to think about beyond first impressions. These words softly detonate in your soul, their lingering causing shifts and changes. Imperceptibly at first, but lasting and seismic over time. Benedictions have that kind of power.

John and I were sitting outside at a park last week. It didn't take long before we heard a familiar refrain: "Dad, watch me!" "Mom, look!"

Our child-rearing behind us, we smiled at each other.

How often had we heard those words? What endless pleasure did our kids seem to get from having us watch when they were doing something they loved? Who would have guessed that there was such power in a face turned toward someone? Just the tilt of the head in the right direction . . .

> The LORD bless you
>   and keep you;
> the LORD make his face shine on you
>   and be gracious to you;
> the LORD turn his face toward you
>   and give you peace.

NUMBERS 6:24-26

Notes

INTRODUCTION
1. See Numbers 6:25; Psalm 31:16, Psalm 67:1.
2. See Genesis 1:1-3; Psalm 119:105, 130; Psalm 36:9; Psalm 104:2; Matthew 5:14-16; John 8:12.

CHAPTER 2: THE SHADOW OF DEATH
1. Personal conversation with Dallas Willard.
2. See Matthew 9:30; Mark 1:43; 14:6.

CHAPTER 10: BEFORE THE DAWN
1. Job 6:2-3, 15; 7:3-4, 6-7, 15-16; 10:1; 16:16; 30:27.
2. Personal conversation with Dallas Willard.

CHAPTER 12: GLIMMERS
1. Matthew 5:3, 6, 10; Luke 6:27, 29.

About the Author

NANCY ORTBERG served as a teaching pastor for eight years at Willow Creek Community Church in South Barrington, Illinois. During that time she led Network, a ministry that helps people identify their spiritual gifts and find a place of service in the church, and Axis, a weekly gathering for the eighteen- to twenty-something generation.

She is a founding partner of Teamworx2, a business and leadership consulting firm affiliated with Patrick Lencioni, which provides fast-paced, practical, and compelling sessions to leaders and their teams. Teamworx2 works with businesses, schools, nonprofits, and churches to address issues of organizational effectiveness and teamwork. Nancy is currently on staff at Menlo Park Presbyterian Church as the Director of Leadership Development, where she is working to create a dynamic and innovative approach to leadership development.

Nancy is a gifted communicator who is passionate about helping people connect what they believe with their everyday lives. A highly sought-after speaker, Nancy has been a featured presenter at the Catalyst and Orange conferences, and has been a regular contributor to *Rev! Magazine*.

Nancy is the author of *Looking for God: Slightly Unorthodox, Highly Unconventional, and Entirely Unexpected Thoughts about Faith* and *Unleashing the Power of Rubber Bands: Lessons in Non-Linear Leadership*.

She and her husband, John, live in the Bay Area and have three grown children: Laura, Mallory, and Johnny.

FOR MORE FROM NANCY, ENJOY THE FOLLOWING EXCERPTS FROM *LOOKING FOR GOD*.

Nancy Ortberg is not like Most-of-Us. At least, she's not like the Most-of-Us that experts tell us we are supposed to be. Because she's not like Most-of-Us, she's got something to say to All-of-Us.

SCOT McKNIGHT
Author of *The Jesus Creed*

Looking for God

slightly unorthodox,

highly unconventional, and entirely unexpected

thoughts about faith

NANCY ORTBERG

THEPROBLEM**WITH**
QUIET TIME

For most of my growing up years, I heard about the daily "quiet time."

It was revered and talked about as the bedrock of the Christian faith. It was described as a serene and profound time in the morning (anything less than thirty minutes was quite unworthy) when one sat alone with God in meditation and study over a passage in Scripture. It also included a time of prayer (usually following an acronym like *ACTS:* Adoration, Confession, Thanksgiving, Supplication . . . and we do not supplicate before we adore) and journaling.

After you had one—people always say they've "had" their quiet times—you talked about it. You might sneak it into a conversation in a way that was seemingly unpretentious, but always comparative. You'd talk about what a deep time you'd had that morning alone with God. How God had spoken to you. What a meaningful insight you'd received over a particular passage in the Bible. How long you had lingered over your journal that day.

And other people made sure to ask you about it in order to "hold you accountable."

"How is your time with God going? What is He teaching you?"

Quiet time was always the barometer for your relationship with God, the ultimate measurement of your devotion and maturity. It was as if your whole relationship with God hinged on that morning experience.

So for many years, I practiced my quiet time. Not quite daily, but close—and whenever I missed a day, I was filled with great consternation and guilt. Every day, I expected something profound to occur during my quiet time, but most days, nothing approached profound. And when I engaged in conversation with others about our quiet times, my experience never quite lived up to theirs.

Then there came a point in my life when for a number of years, "quiet time" wasn't an option. Now, you may disagree with that last sentence, but this is my book, and I am telling you, during that period I could not have done a quiet time if I'd had a gun to my head.

My daughter Laura was three, Mallory was only eighteen months, and I was pregnant with Johnny. Never was there a more oxymoronic phrase than "quiet time." In those days, I had to fight to go to the bathroom by myself, and when I did make it in there alone, one or both kids were always on the other side of the door, pounding and calling to me.

"Mommy, can we come in?"

"No."

"Mommy, when are you coming out?"

"In a minute."

"Mommy, is a minute up?"

I had never known before what it was like to wake up tired. Disrupted by teething and ear infections, my nights were staccato notes of sleep. When I woke up, the kids were either crying to be fed or unrolling toilet paper from the bathroom down the hall and wrapping the cat.

Days and weeks would go by without a moment for me to sit and open the Bible. And when those moments came, I either lost my train of thought or I fell asleep! But quiet time had been presented to me as the main/only means of connecting deeply to God, so I panicked. During this early stage of motherhood, I desperately needed God, but I was unable to connect with Him in the only way I thought counted.

I figured I could either meet with God again in about six years (when all of the kids would be in school) or I would have to find other ways to connect to Him. And I did not know any other ways.

But God did.

I was standing in my kitchen trying to decide what to fix for dinner. Laura and Mallory were playing on the carpet but growing increasingly fussy after a long day. I was about twelve months pregnant, and exhausted.

I had an idea. We still had some time before dinner needed to be a reality, so I threw the girls in their car seats and headed off to the park, hoping they could work off some energy before I had to start dinner. (I also thought this could buy me more time to figure out *what* we would be having for dinner.)

I found a park bench I could sit on while the girls played, although I was so big I wasn't sure I would be able to jump up quickly if one of them needed something. I didn't really have a plan other than to let them play for about thirty minutes before heading home.

God's plan was to show me a window.

I watched as the girls dug in the sand and skipped around trying to catch the ducks. The sun was warm and low in the sky and provided me a sort of silhouetted view of my little redheaded daughters. I sat for a moment, relaxing into that scene, when all of a sudden I was so very deeply struck by how much I loved those kids. This wasn't just a recognition that I loved them but a very unexpected, visceral response. While I had been mostly frustrated up to this point, as I sat on that bench watching them play and squeal with delight, I felt as if my heart would just burst with the amount of love it held for those two little girls. I found myself fighting back the tears, feeling a tightening in my throat and an overwhelming sense of this deep emotion for my children.

Almost in that same moment, when my defenses were

down and I was flooded with intense emotion, God sent a tsunami that absolutely blindsided me. He whispered to me, *And that's just the tip of the iceberg as to how much I love you.*

Now I realize that most people would be really grateful to have an experience like this, and they'd probably respond really well. But for some reason, my heart just didn't seem to have enough room to accept this message God was trying to give me. My mind didn't have the capacity to understand it. In that one sentence, there seemed to be more goodness and grace than my body could contain.

And it was simply too much to take in, so I said aloud, "Stop!"

I am sure more than one person passing by wondered why this twelve-month-pregnant woman was talking to herself at the park. Tears welling up in my eyes, I scooped up the girls, put them into the car, and drove home. Now, not only did I still have no clue what to fix for dinner, I also did not know what to do with this whisper from God.

When he wrote to the Ephesian church, Paul said he prayed for them that they might have the power to understand just how wide, how long, how high, and how deep God's love is (Ephesians 3:18). I find it fascinating that he should pray not just that they would understand the vastness of God's love, but that God would give them the power necessary to grasp it.

In the days that followed, that moment on the park bench would not leave me, and I found myself thinking about it often. Over time, I began to understand that much of my heart was Teflon coated. It was protecting itself from getting hurt, but in the process it had also became impervious to what it really needed. God had used a moment when I was most open to overwhelm and break through that coating with what my heart needed. God knew that I needed a deep understanding of the kind of love He had for me. But it felt so foreign to me that when I experienced it, "Stop!" was my first reaction. How funny to yell stop at what you most need.

The walls of my limited understanding of love had trapped me. But God cut a little hole in my wall—a window—and gave me a glimpse into the kind of love that He offers. Then He told me that it was just that: a peek. Nowhere close to the fullness of His love. And even the glimpse, at least initially, was too much for me. Sometimes windows are like that. We move rapidly away from what we see in them, only to be drawn back to the view.

I knew that I was not fully ready to comprehend the extent to which God had revealed His love to me that day, but I also realized something else. It had been a very long time since I had felt that deeply connected to the presence of God. There had been weeks and months of quiet times when I never experienced God like that. I had read verses and journaled about those verses and even talked with other people about those verses, but I had never been *that* aware of God. The encounter I had with God on that park bench went beyond any experience I had ever had during a quiet time.

God began to teach me that there were so very many ways to deepen my relationship with Him. So very many ways in which to know and experience Him. And that the park bench *counted* as much as the quiet time did. That was revolutionary for me.

Slowly I began to understand that I had been seeing God from such a narrow perspective. I had boxed God up and compartmentalized Him into thirty minutes each morning. But in reality, He had been waiting for me to realize that He had invaded all the parts of my day, if I would just pay attention.

So I began to have "quiet times" all over the place.

Not long after this, my husband, John, and I went to see the stage production of *Les Misérables.* Toward the end of the play, as the hero, Jean Valjean, is near death, he sings to his adopted daughter, Cosette, "to love another person is to see the face of God."

As I watched the scene, tears began streaming down my face. I am not by nature a big crier, so John quickly asked me what was wrong. I said, "That is one of the truest and most beautiful phrases I have ever heard. That should have been a verse in the Bible. Why didn't God make that a verse in the Bible?"

One night, a few weeks later, John got into bed and said, "I want to read you something."

He opened his Bible to Genesis 33 and read to me the words of Jacob, reunited with Esau after having been estranged for a long time: "For to see your face is like seeing the face of God" (verse 10).

I was so glad to see that God had taken me up on my suggestion to make that a verse in the Bible.

And after that, often when I was in conversation with a good friend, I would think that part of the experience was like looking into the face of God: a quiet time.

Whenever I ate a good meal, preferably one I did not have to cook, I was struck by the gratuitous nature of the God who made the colors, flavors, and textures of avocado, red pepper, and tilapia. He only needed to make food nutritious and caloric. Everything we eat could simply taste like bread and milk, and functionally that would be good enough. There is really no need for the variety and taste sensations that we experience when we eat, but God created them anyway. Steve Evans, a noted Christian philosopher, says that perhaps the best proof for the existence of God is banana cream pie. I think Steve is onto something.

So just as I found God in my friendships and in my children, I realized that a meal could also become a quiet time. Through my awareness of and gratitude for oatmeal with brown sugar, figs, and oranges, or mixed green lettuce and mushrooms, or horseradish sauce on a thinly sliced filet, I deeply reflected on the good nature of God. I truly learned what it means to "taste and see that the LORD is good" (Psalm 34:8).

We get so prescriptive with the spiritual life. We prepackage what it means to have quiet time, and then we duplicate it, mass-produce it, insist upon it, and brag about it. We make it a formula: Thirty minutes. In the morning. Prayer that includes adoration, confession, thanksgiving, and supplication. And then, of course, we journal.

I remember where I was the day I realized that Jesus never

journaled. I was driving, and when that thought flashed through my mind, I challenged it. *That can't be true.* When I realized it was true—*Jesus never journaled*—I pulled my car over to the side of the road and couldn't figure out whether to laugh or cry.

I don't think journaling is bad. I just think we have come to see it as a spiritual necessity, and it's not. My husband is a pretty consistent journaler. It is very helpful to him in connecting with God. It is a practice that has helped shape his relationship and response to God. It is not so with me. I find journaling tedious. I am very self-conscious when I do it. I fall into the trap of doing it just to keep the dates consistent. I worry that when I die, someone will open those journals and notice the enormous gaps between the dates. John suggested that I pencil in "see other journals for missing entries," but I figured if I had to lie about my spiritual practice it might be time to find a new one.

I also don't think having a quiet time is bad. Quite the contrary. Quiet times have helped me enrich my relationship with God and transform my character. But when it becomes prescriptive and confining and routine, a quiet time can be more of a barrier than a help.

There are so many correlations in Scripture between the spiritual life and the life of an athlete in training. As followers of Christ, we need to cross train. Athletes do this so that the whole body is developed, not just a focused part of it. When we give ourselves permission to vary our spiritual routines, we emerge with a broader, multifaceted view of our great

God. What a joy to realize that from the time we wake up in the morning until the moment we lay our head on the pillow to sleep, we have been given a variety of extraordinary ways to connect with our extraordinary God.

Not long ago, we were driving on the highway that goes into Yosemite through the Wawona Tunnel. When we emerged from the tunnel, we came to a spot on the left where we could pull over: Inspiration Point. Scores of cars were parked there, and people were getting out of their cars to take photographs.

We got out of the car, and suddenly I was overwhelmed by one of the most magnificent views I had ever seen. The valley below was truly awe-inspiring, with El Capitan's sheer granite wall on the left, and Half Dome and Bridal Veil Falls on the right. There was no sign telling people to whisper, but intuitively, they were. It seemed that we were all in awe as we witnessed what can happen with a wave of God's hand.

As I looked down into the valley, I was reminded that a very big God is taking care of the universe. And all of this goes on while I am occupied with my simple little life. The beauty that He has created is absolutely breathtaking, and it is only a glimpse at the beauty of His Spirit.

And for me, it is a quiet time.

And it *counts*.

HOLY

I'VE NEVER MUCH CARED for the word *holy*. A lot of other words that describe God—*loving, powerful, omnipresent*—I'm good with.

Holy. That one has always been hard for me. It has always made God seem so distant, a bit angry, even "holier-than-thou." I know what you're thinking, but still.

And it's not a word we use much, except when we are talking about God or swearing.

Sometime right around February 1990 I changed how I felt about that word. For a number of months we had known my dad was dying—pancreatic cancer. He had wasted down to ninety pounds and was turning yellow. Although he had fought valiantly, there came a point when we knew there would be no winning. A very wise person told me, "Now it's time to help him die well."

February 14 is Valentine's Day, and February 16 is my parents' wedding anniversary. My dad died on February 15. Mom called and said that the nurses had told her to call us, so my husband and I got to the hospital around 6 p.m. It was not the first time we had gotten a call like that, but as soon as we made it to his room, we knew it would be the last.

Mom was exhausted from hours at his bedside—hours that had come at the end of an eighteen-month battle with cancer. We told her to go home for a while and that we would stay with Dad.

He was semiconscious for the first hour or so, and I used the opportunity to talk into his ear, mostly telling him things I remembered about growing up as his daughter. I definitely reminded him about the lizards.

After a couple of hours, he slipped into a coma and stopped responding to my touch and voice. His breathing changed, and his hands and feet started getting cold. As his body began to prepare for death, my dad lost control of his bowels. A nurse came in to clean him up, and I stepped to the back of the room. She was so gentle with him, even though she knew he couldn't feel anything, draping the sheet carefully to protect his dignity, even in those last moments.

But as she pulled the sheet back slightly, I caught a glimpse of his back and leg. He was skeletal, and his skin was yellow. The room smelled bad. It was all so wrong.

Rather than reaching the acceptance phase of this death and dying thing—after all, it *had* been eighteen months—I just wanted to scream about how wrong this all was. This was not the way it was supposed to be. He was sixty-two years old. He was planning to take an early retirement, and he and my mom were going to travel. He was the grandfather of a four-and-a-half-year-old, a three-year-old, and a one-year-old. Yet here he was, fifteen minutes from death in a body that had deteriorated so much he was nearly unrecognizable.

That's when it hit me. Holiness, whether I liked it or not, was what I craved. A holy world, a world set right, the way it was supposed to be. Sacred and pure, clean and strong. A holy world, where there is no smog in LA, no cracks in the sidewalk. A holy world where children are never hungry, wars are never fought. No snow in Chicago, no struggles that overtake us, no fathers dying.

Holy.

Holy, holy, holy. I may never fully understand the word, and it may never be my favorite descriptor of God, but now when I sing about it, I mean it. There is a sense of longing in the word now, a longing that defines the word in a way that makes me nod. There is an ache in that word now. Because of the pain, *holy* no longer feels distant or angry or superior. It is a soft, kind word, a word full of promise and hope. A word that cannot be fully realized until there is no death.